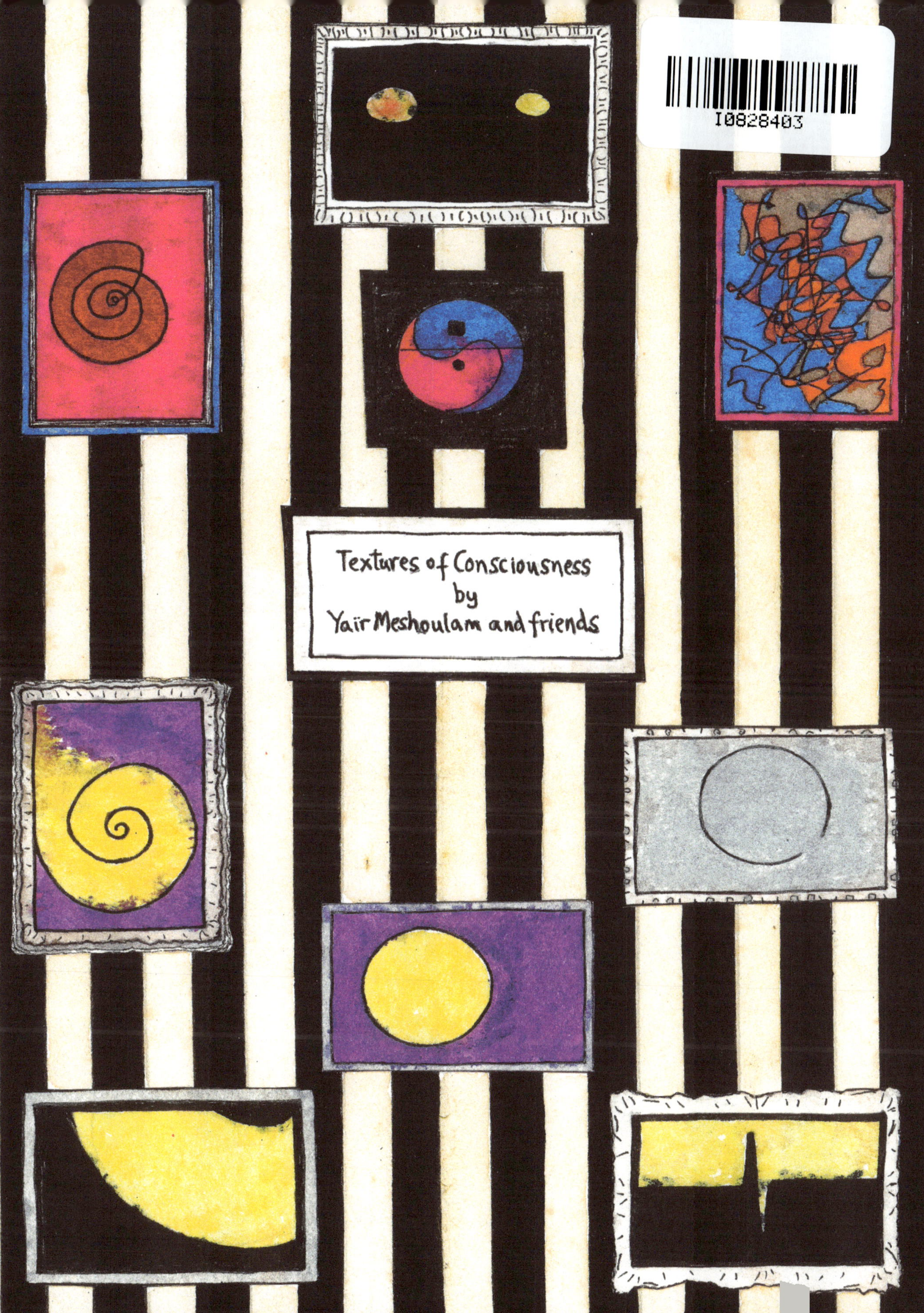
Textures of Consciousness
by
Yaïr Meshoulam and friends
I0828403

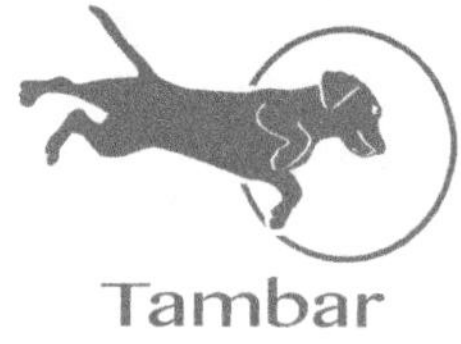

September 2015

Paperback ISBN: 978-1-910133-05-7

Tambar Arts Ltd
e-mail: contact@tambar.co.uk
Reg. No. 03937329
www.tambar.co.uk

Book Design Dylan Martin www.friedbanana.co.uk

A CIP catalogue record for this book is available from the British Library

Contents

'Time is a Texture of Consciousness'

by

Yair Meshoulam

A painting turned into a show, and the show turned into a book.

Things from the mind become objects that inform the mind,

and now that I have posted off the last proof copy of this book,

I would have to look in my computer to see if this all wasn't something I constructed in a dream.

I would like to thank my friends who have contributed their time so generously,

and to you, dear reader, if you exist,

who is about to do the same.

As I was typing the prose

I realised that

it read better as poetry,

so the text is laid out like this

with the expert design wizzardry of Dylan.

All the titles and other details
about the original artworks
are illustrated in the index
at the back of this book

I hope that this book project
can add to the investigation
of
The Textures of Consciousness

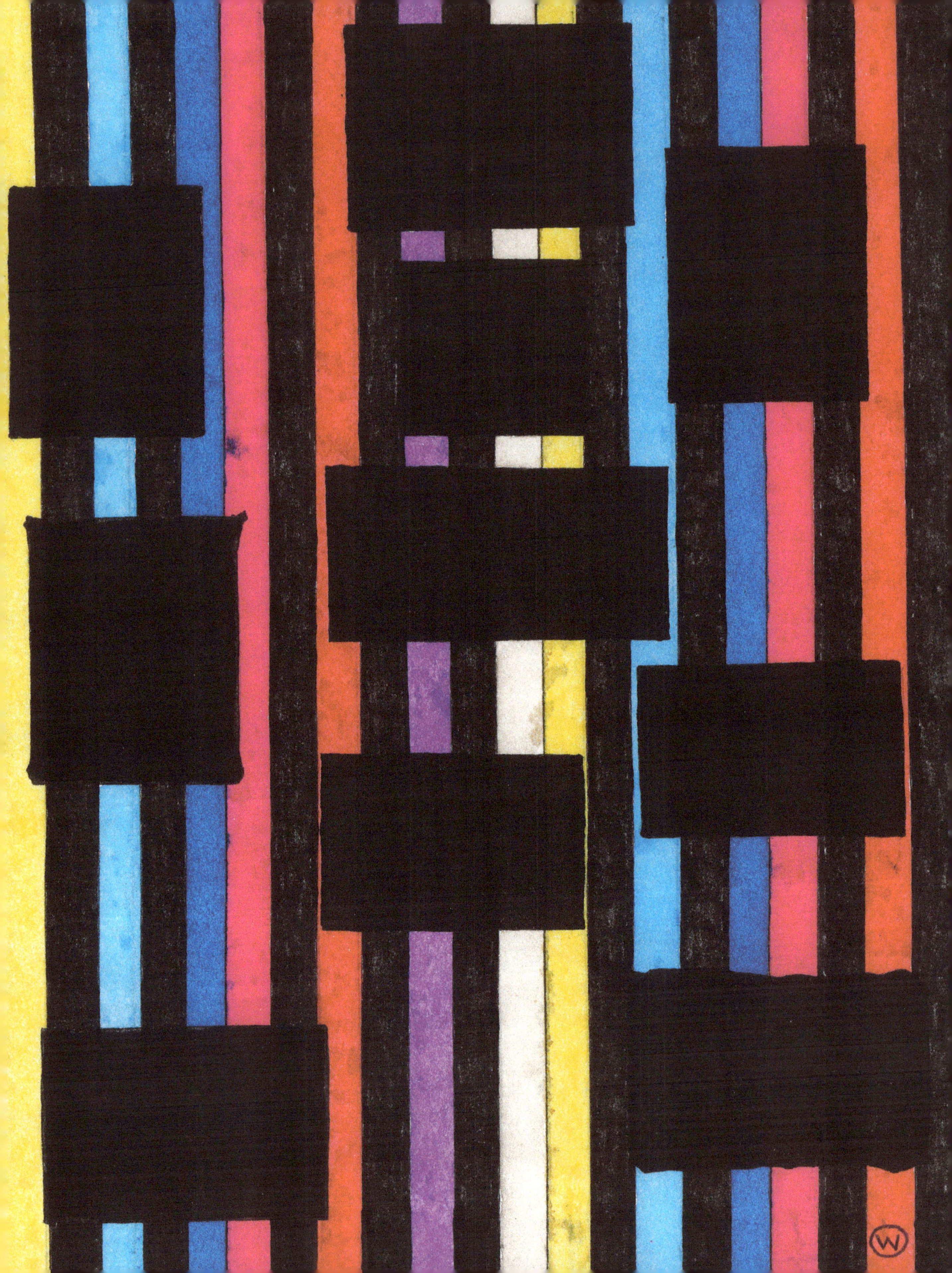

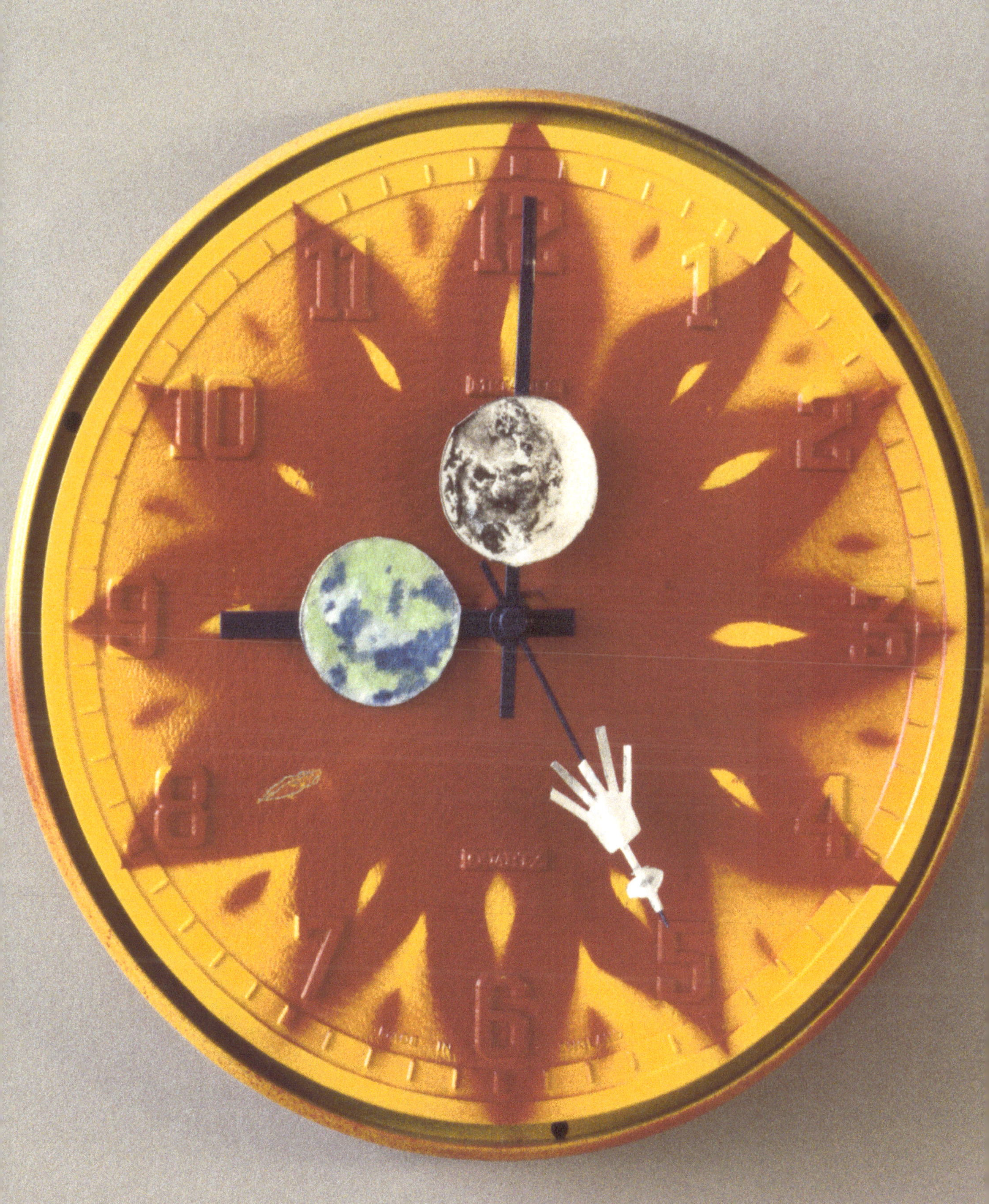

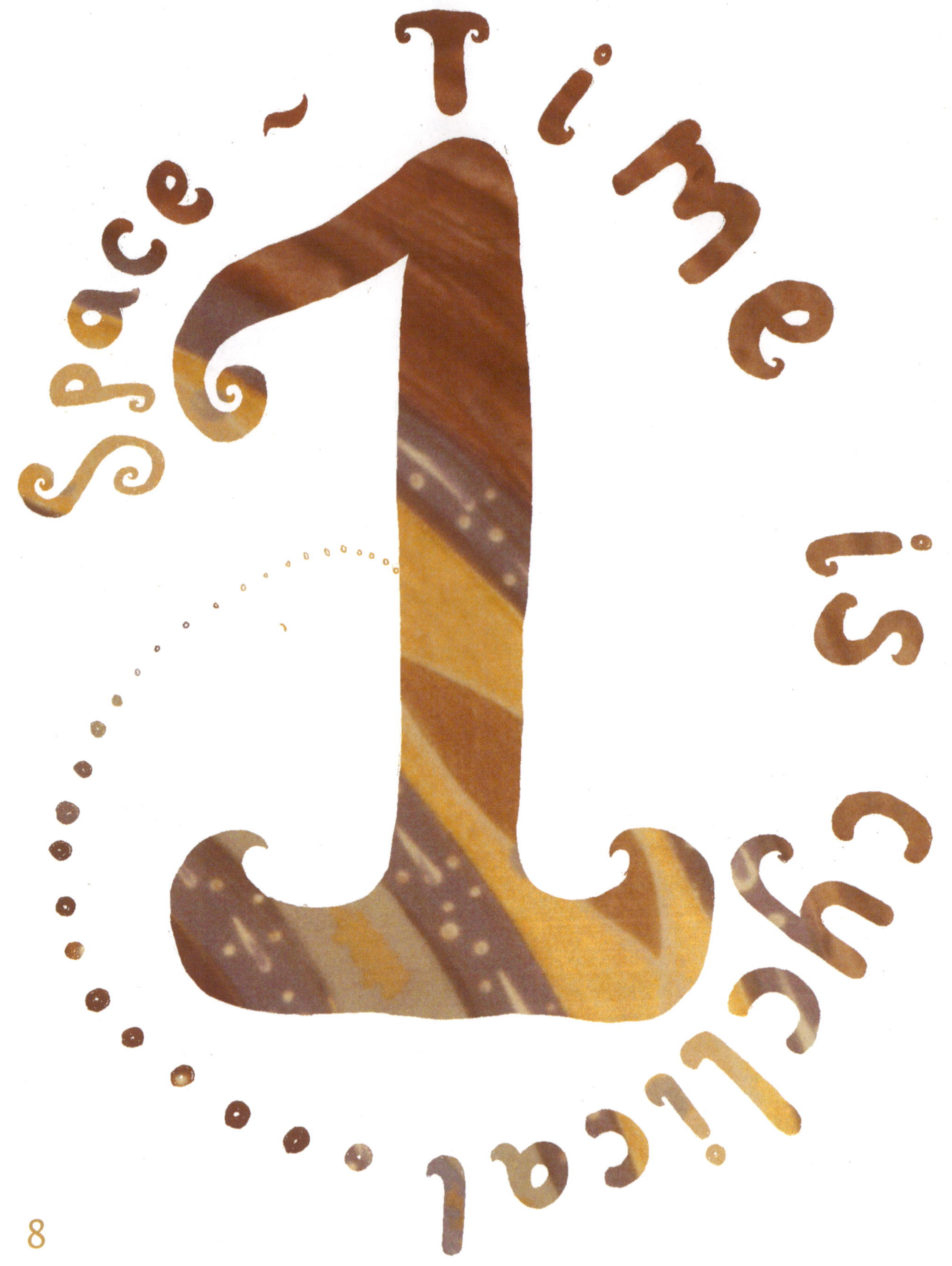
Space-Time is cyclical

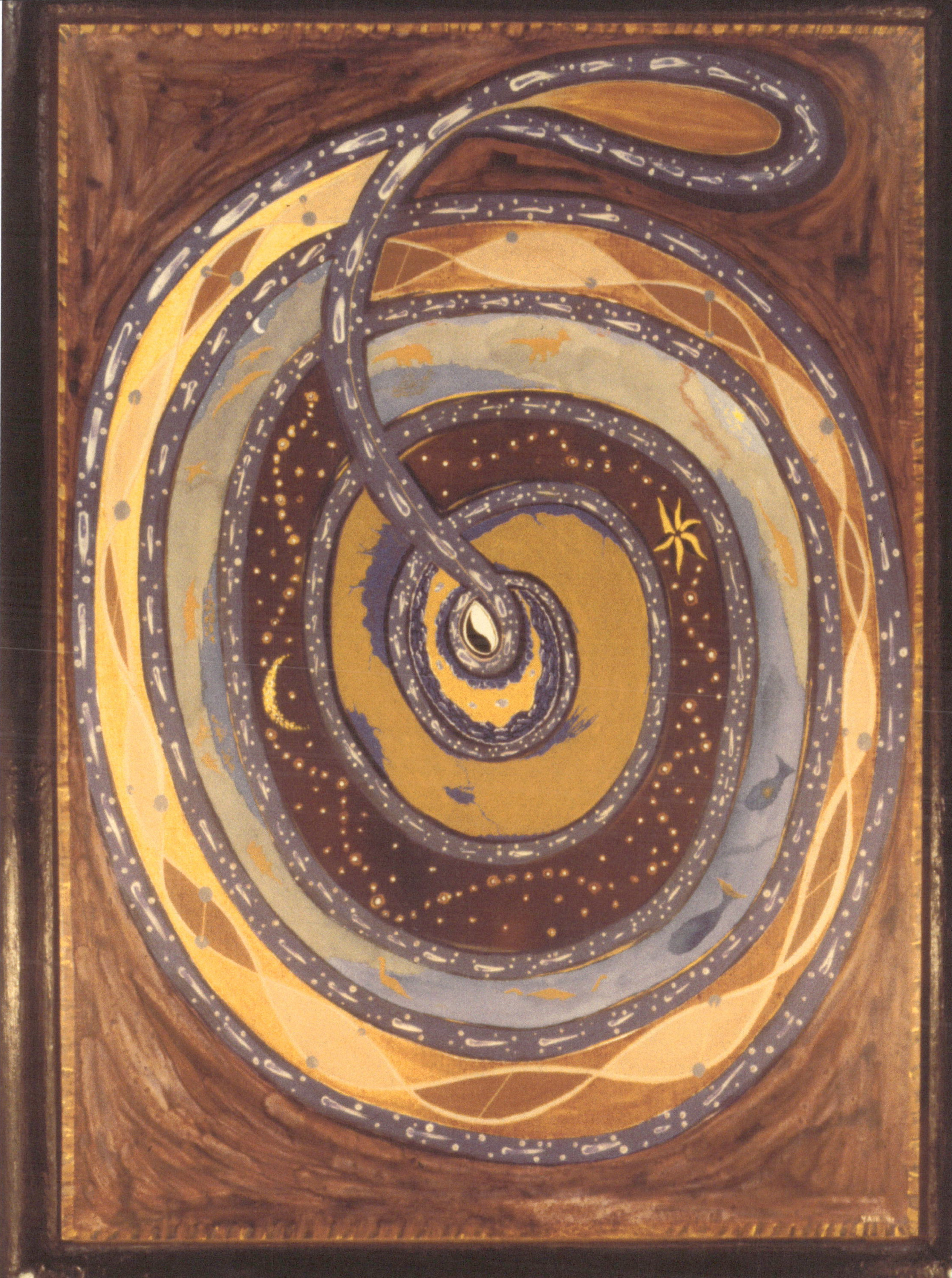

It is interesting to try and work out when exactly is the moment you 'wake up' in the morning.

The moment when your dream world dissolves and you are aware of the world around you -

The moment when you feel conscious.

It might be the sound of the cat scratching at the bedroom door and meowing for their breakfast.

It might be the recognition of a block of light as a tiny gap between the curtains.

It could even be the feel of a pillow against your cheek.

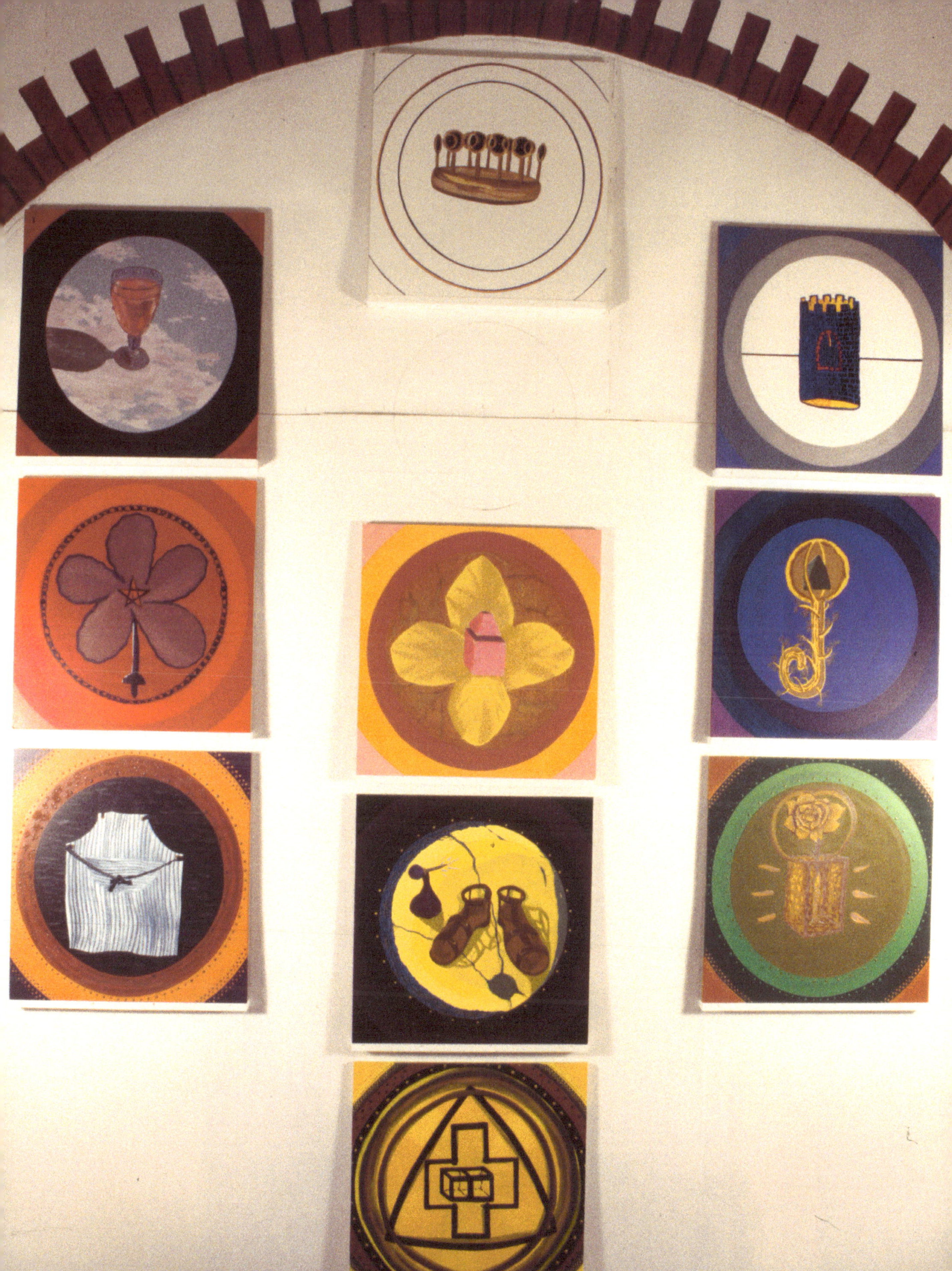

Although I do have a clock by the side of the bed
to check the time,
I find that I wake up at more or less the same
moment
every day.
Probably because my body has its' own
biorythmic clock,
and it is hungry
or thinks it needs coffee, nicotine,
or to urinate.

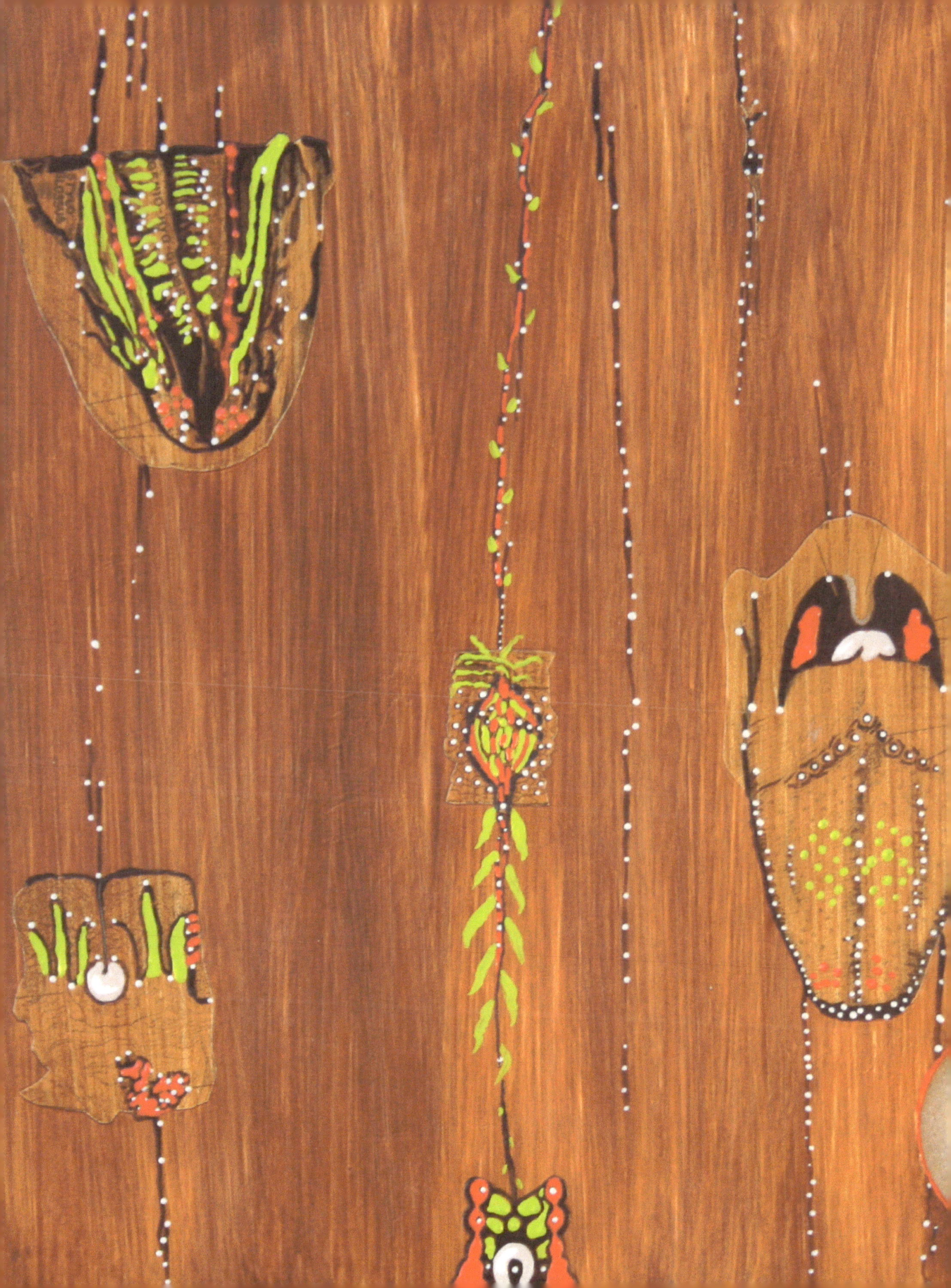

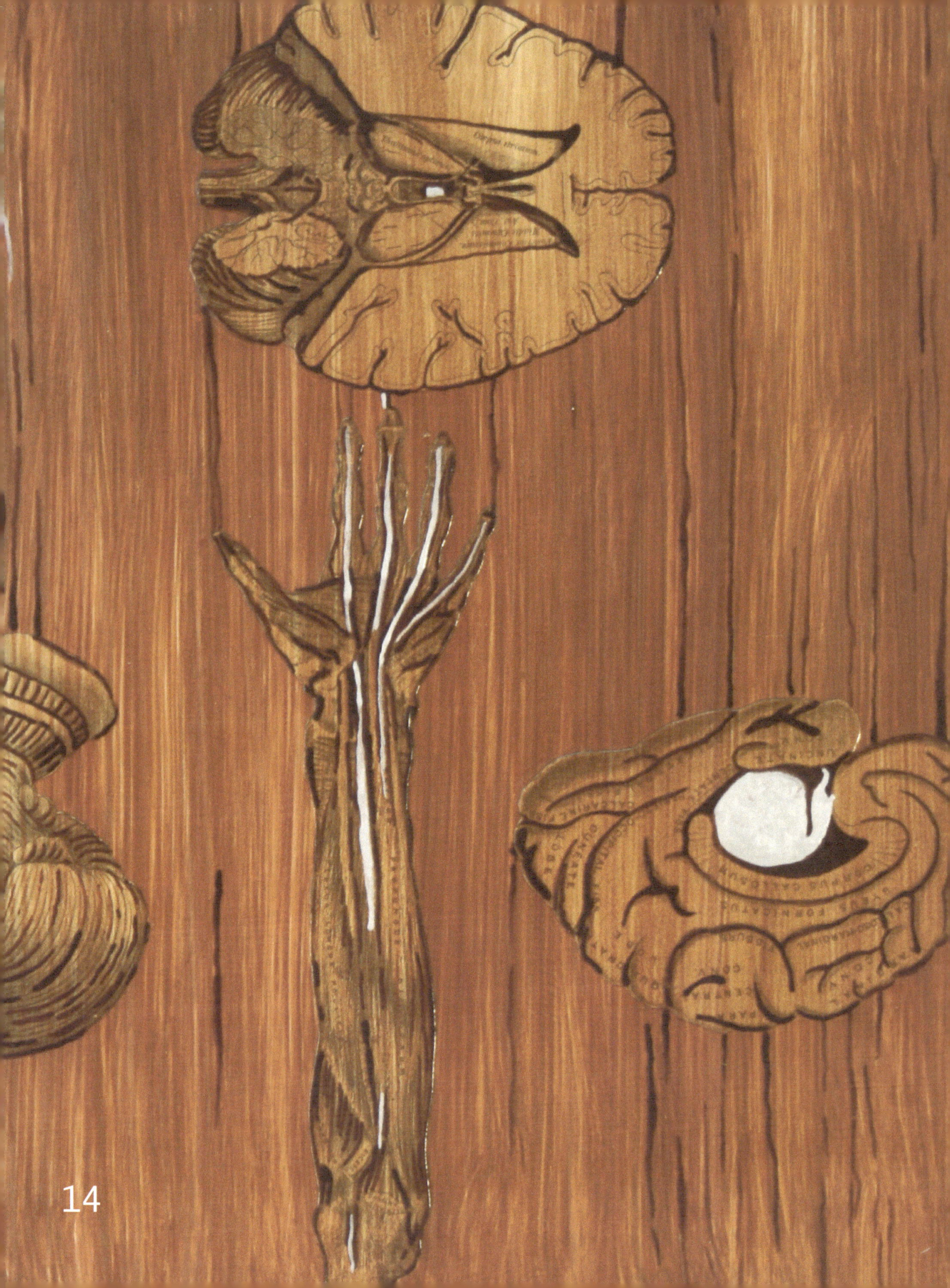

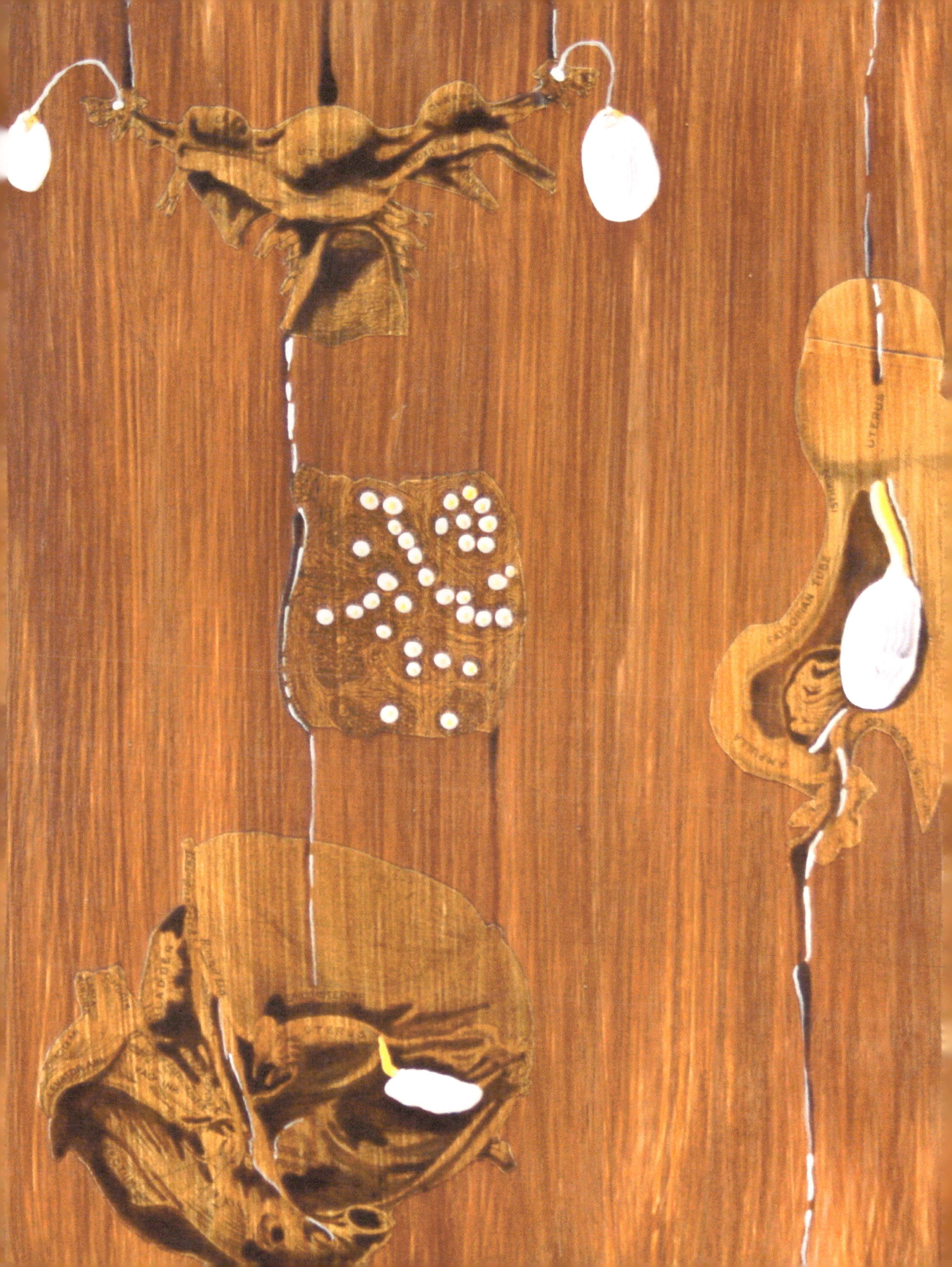
UTERUS
ISTHMUS
FALLOPIAN TUBE

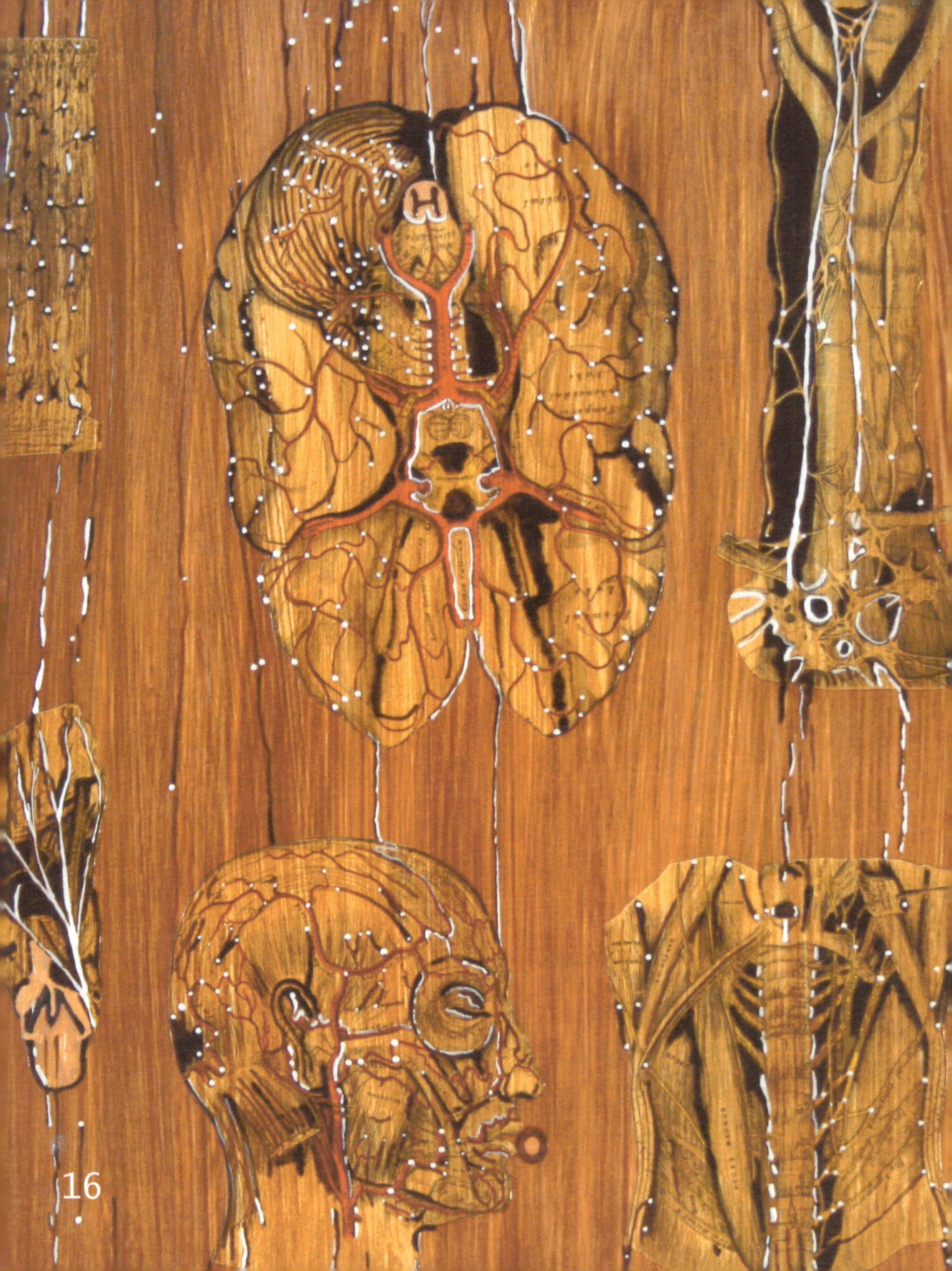

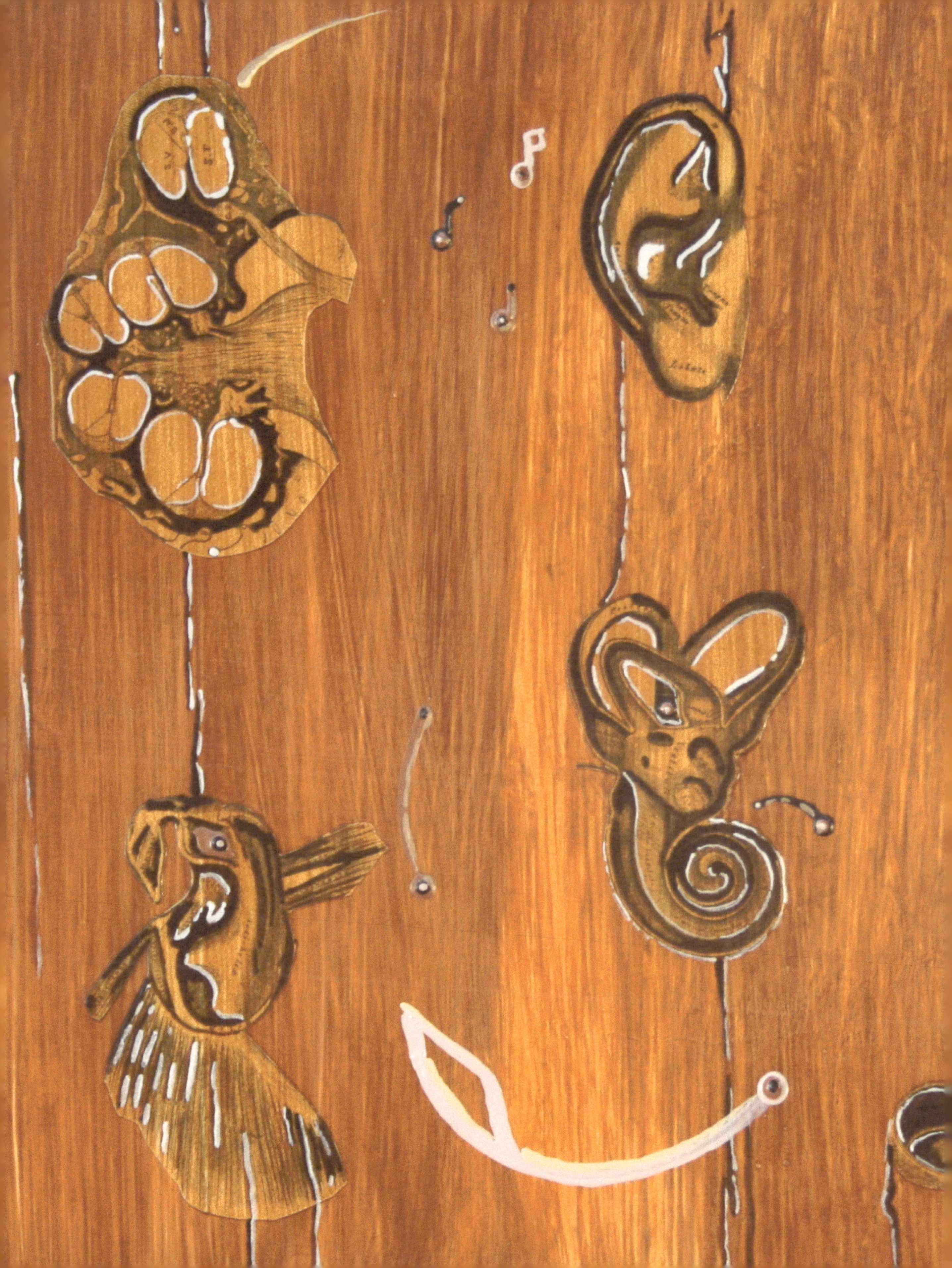

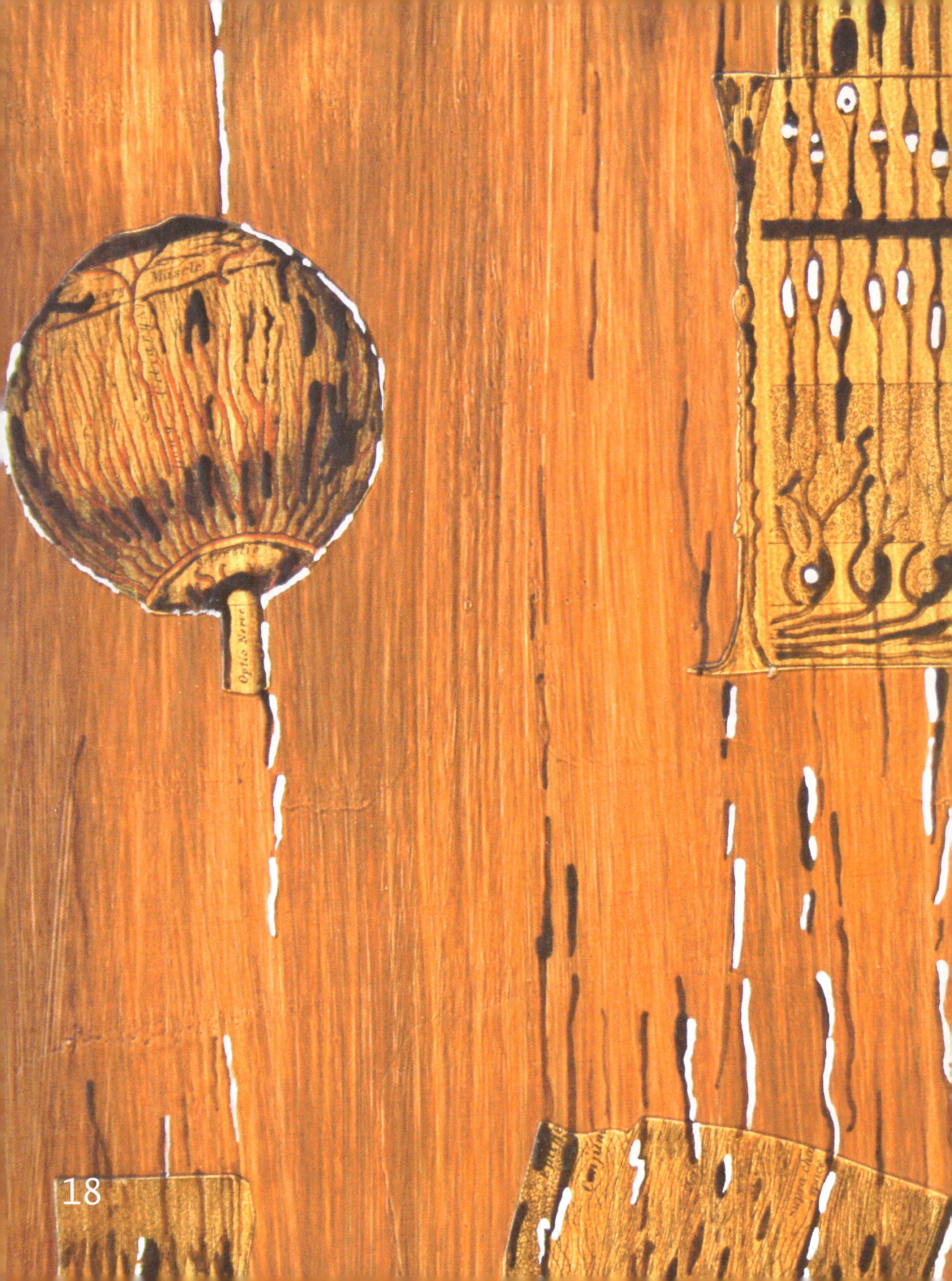
Muscle
Optic Nerve

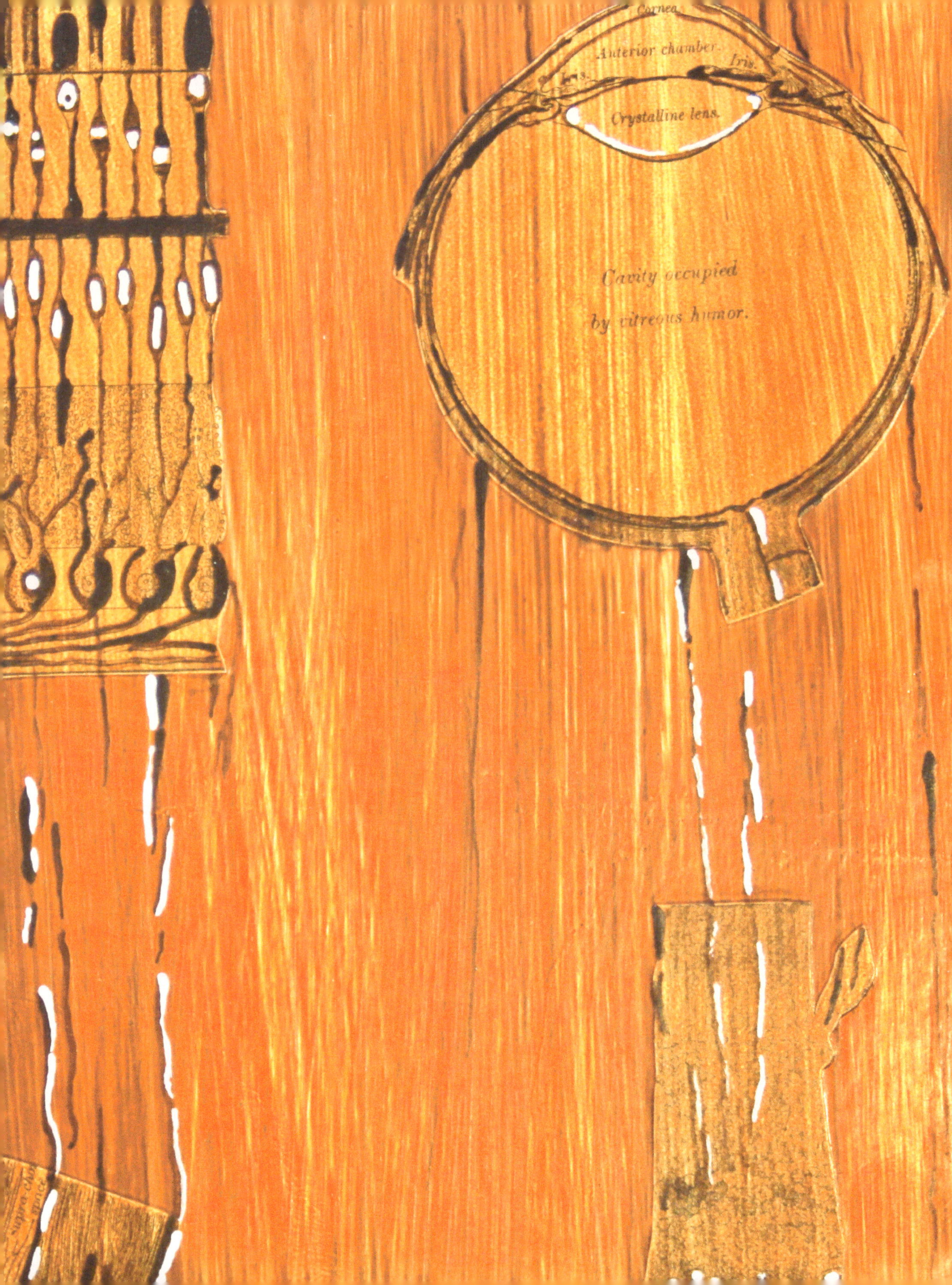
Cornea
Anterior chamber
Iris
Crystalline lens
Cavity occupied
by vitreous humor.

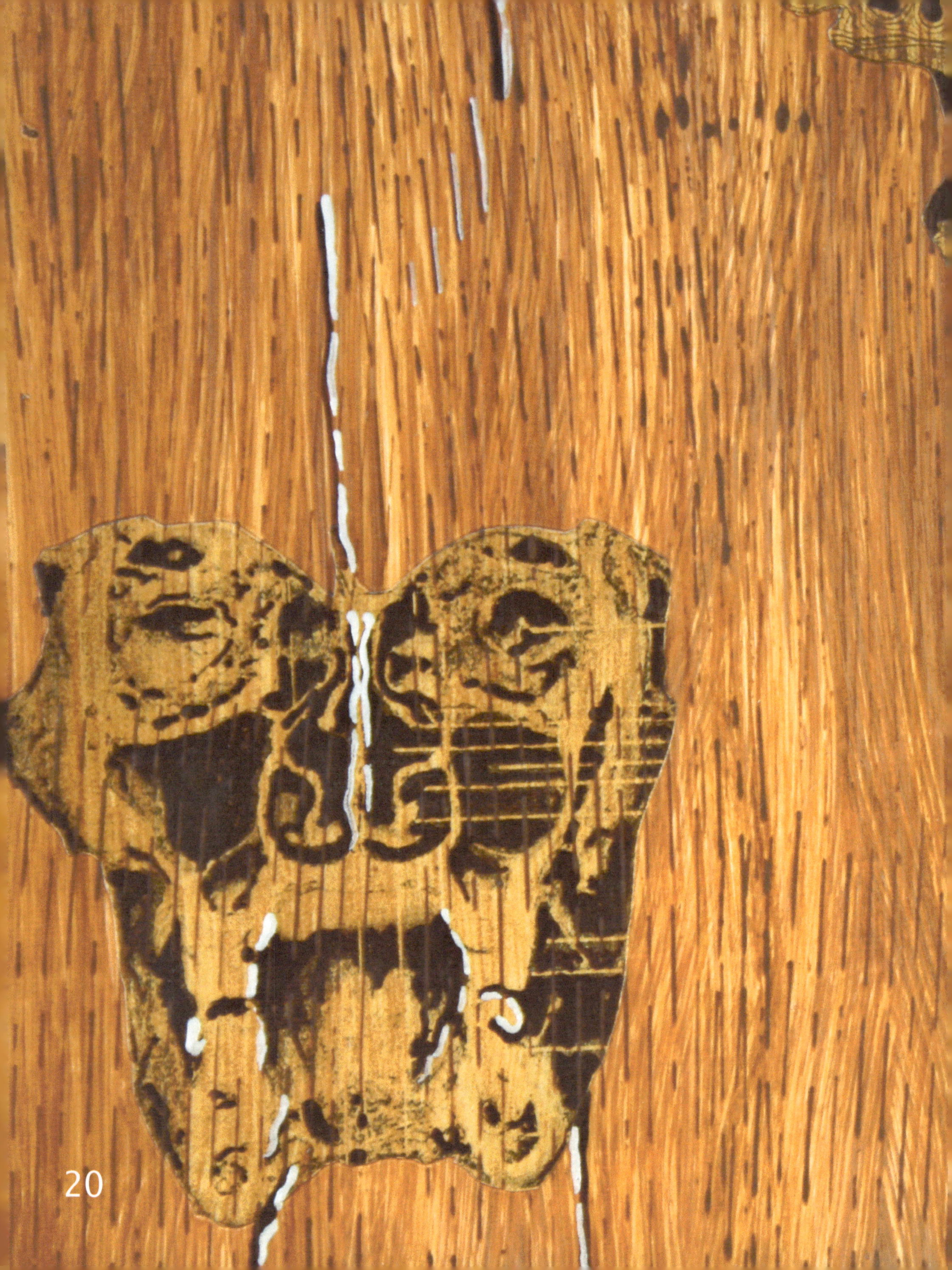

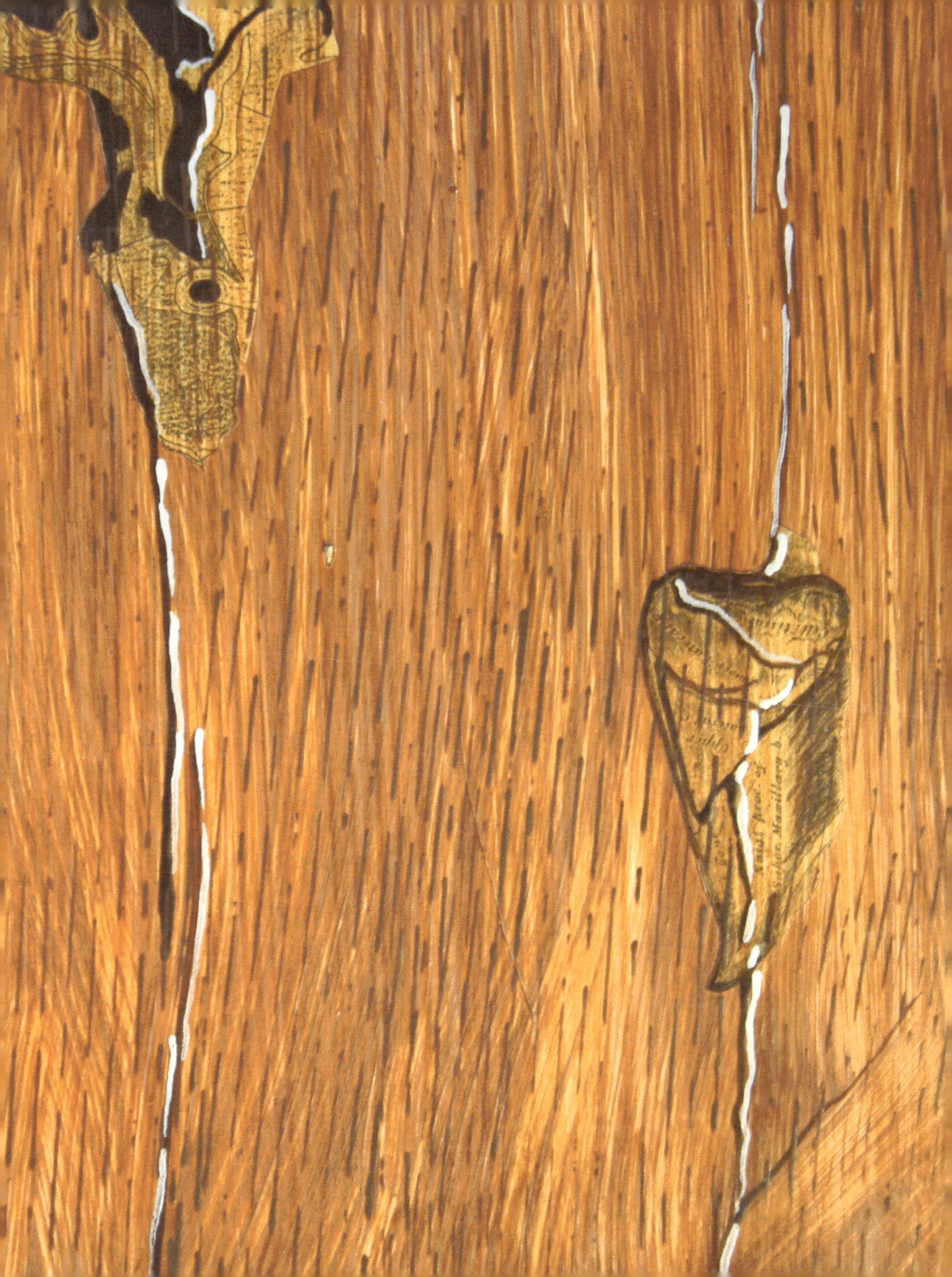

Not only is this sleep-wake pattern cyclical,
or more correctly elliptical,
so it seems is almost everything else around me:

Daylight hours of the day;
months through the year;
season changes
and planetary movement.

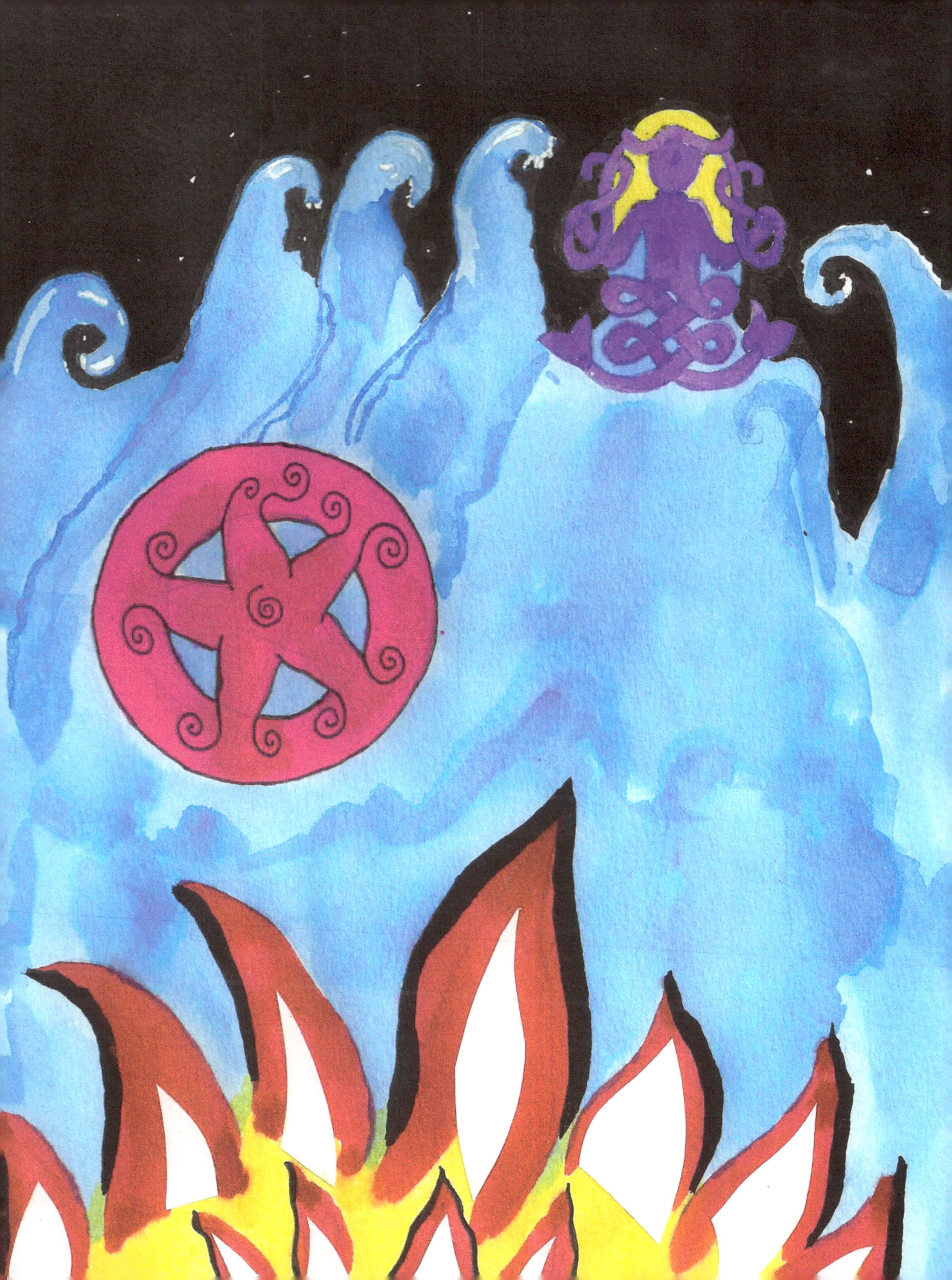

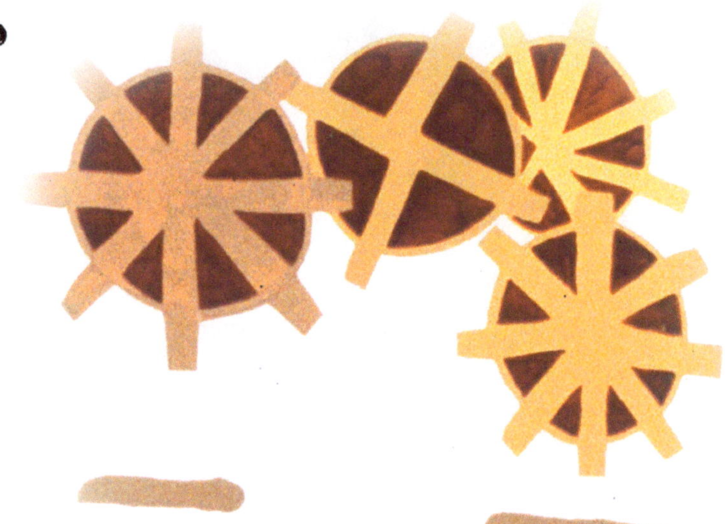

Of course,
I am not the only human to have realised this.
It has been explored from
the ancient Hindu philosophy of reincarnated time
to Fred N's 'Doctrine of Eternal Reoccurrence'.

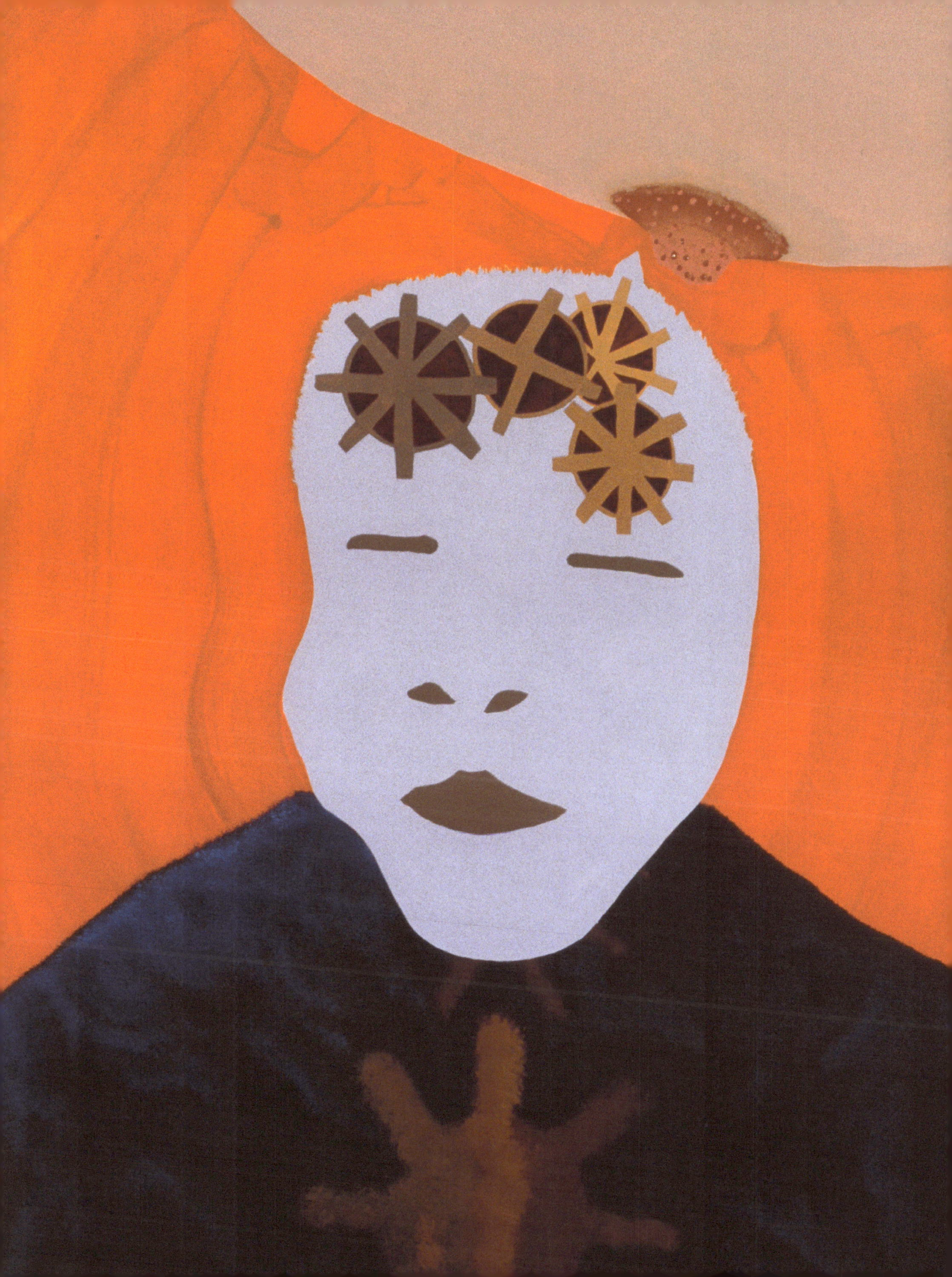

What I like about these more elaborate
constructions of time
is that they uphold the idea
That everything is happening again
and we are just aware,
to varying degrees,
of it going on now.

Of course,
this carries all sorts of questions
about the authorship of your own actions
and what might be the reasons for the
the
path
you
tread.

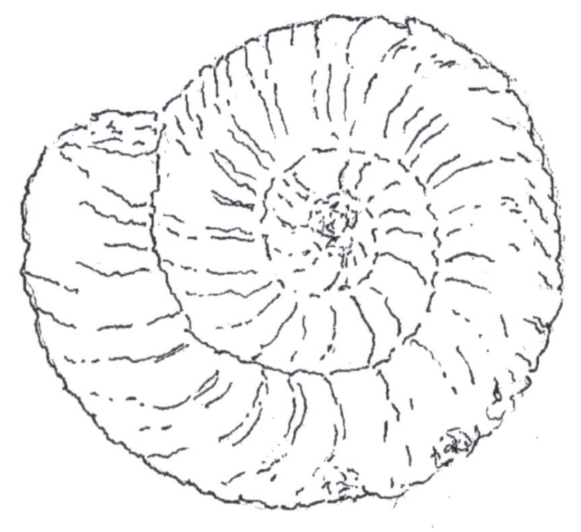

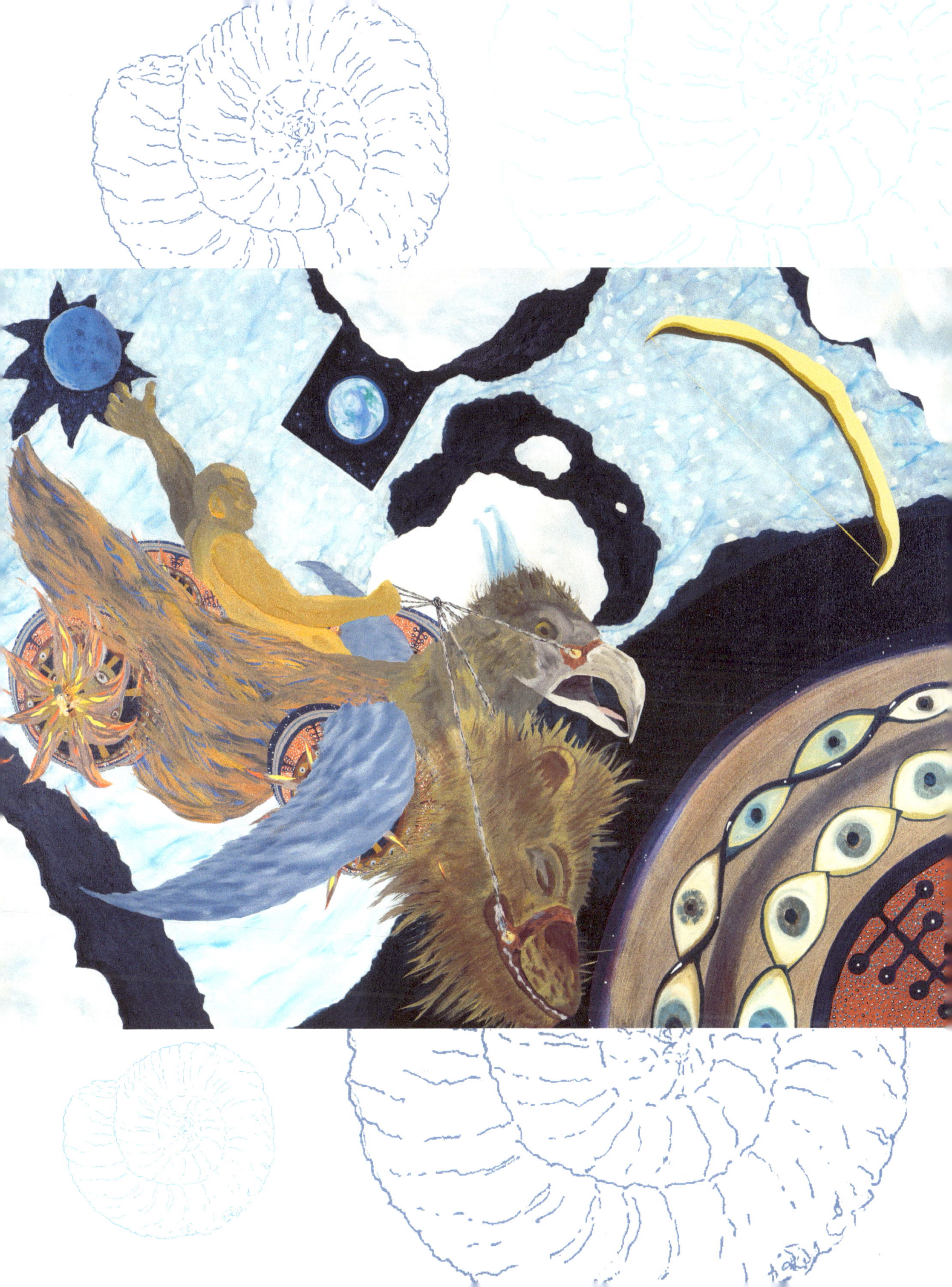

This might even be the 'Eternal Life'
that is so often referred to
in the New Testament,
not some place you go after you die,
but what you live
when you are here and aware of it.

The 'Here and Hereafter'
has a different texture
if you think that
Space-Time is cyclical.

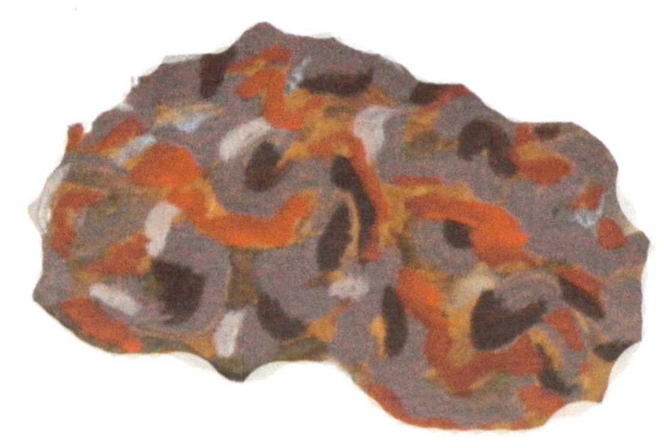

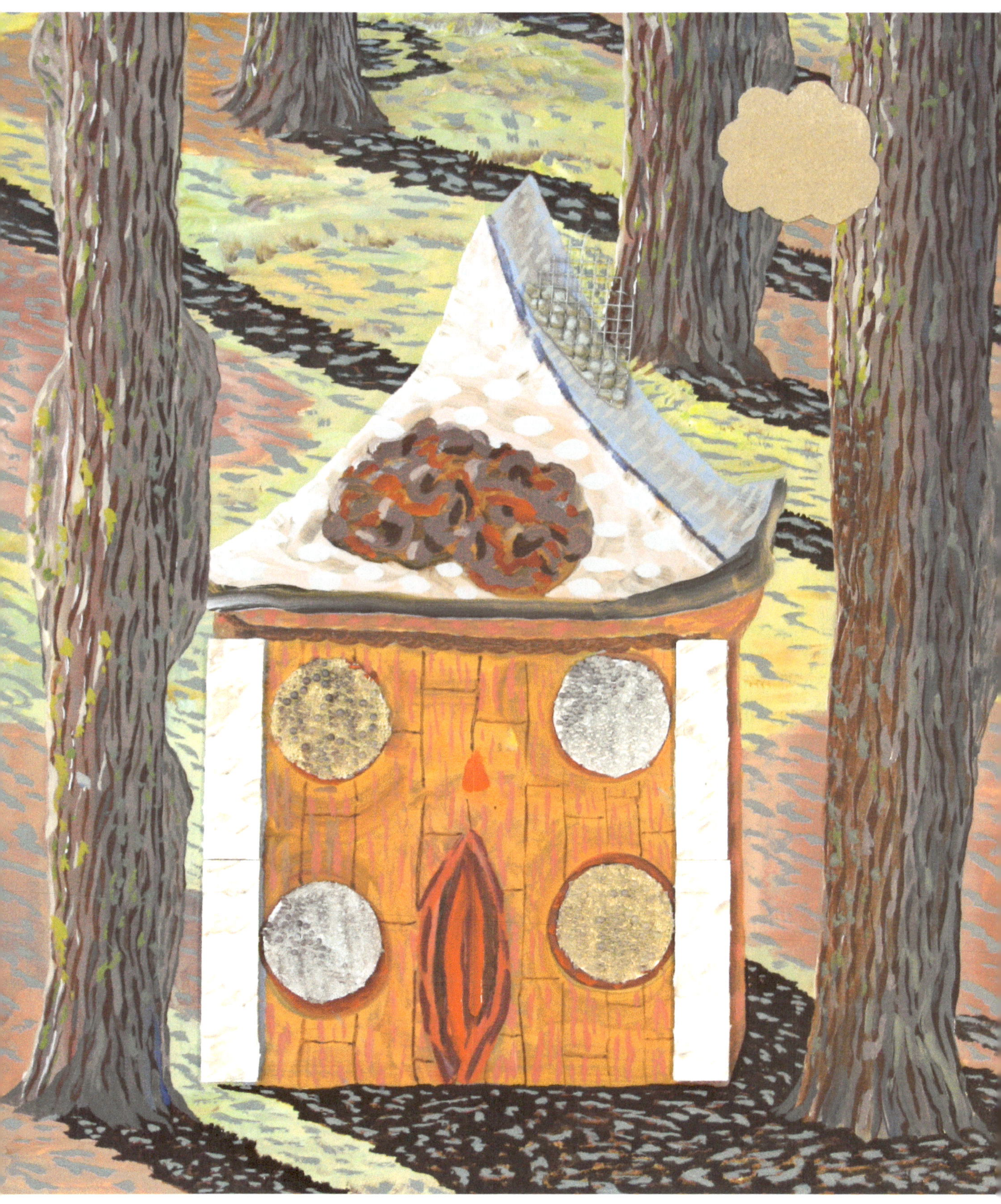

Conversely,
if stuff just happens once
and you move off into a future that goes on forever,
you might arrive at quite a morally neutral position,
which could feel a little blank.

Somewhere that is
beyond good and evil,
e x i s t e n t i a l
or even
a moment
of blissful enlightenment.

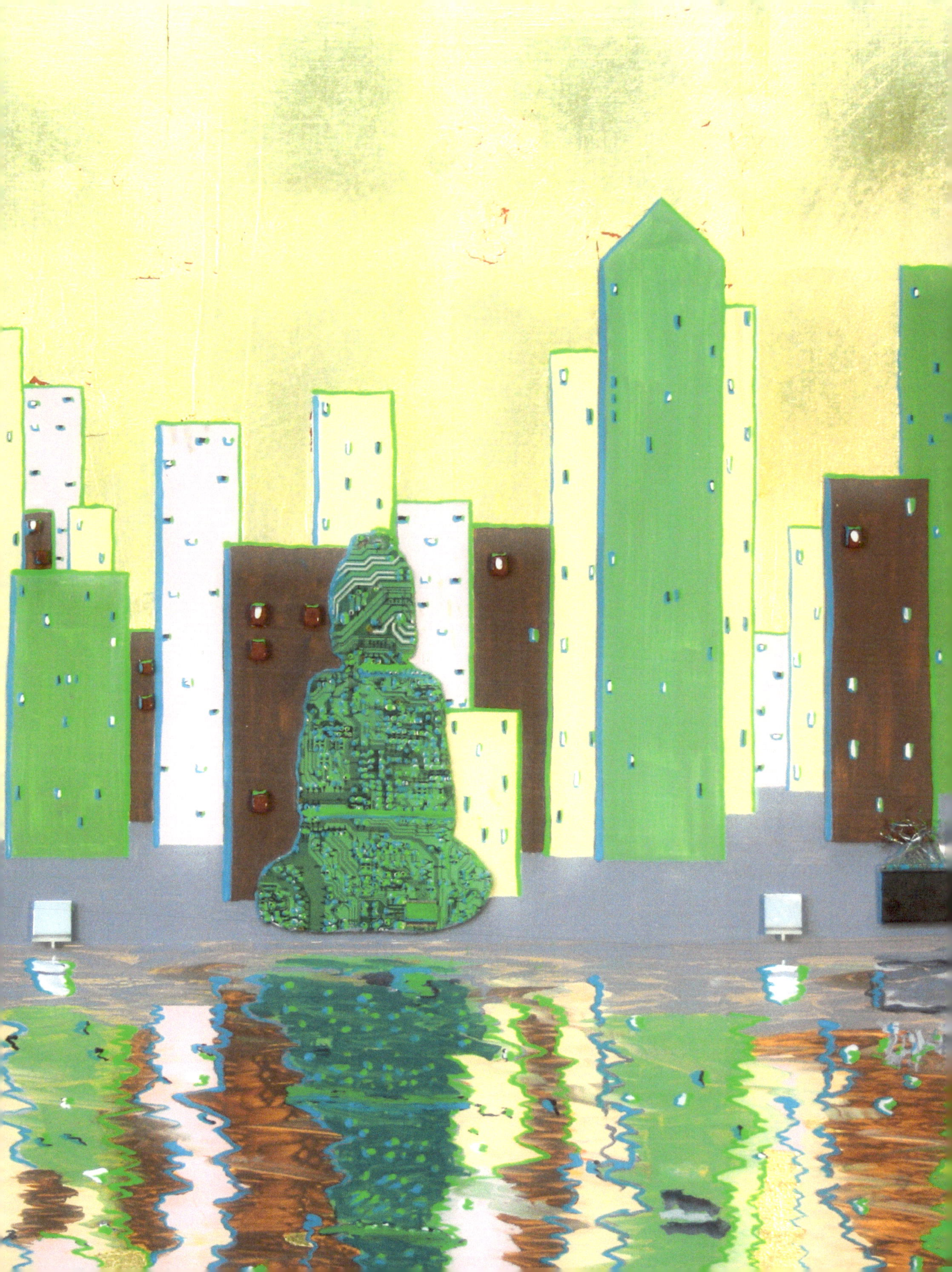

...Needless to say,
if you are convicted of murder,
then the consequences of your actions would be imprisonment,
and that would reoccur eternally,
if time were cyclical.......

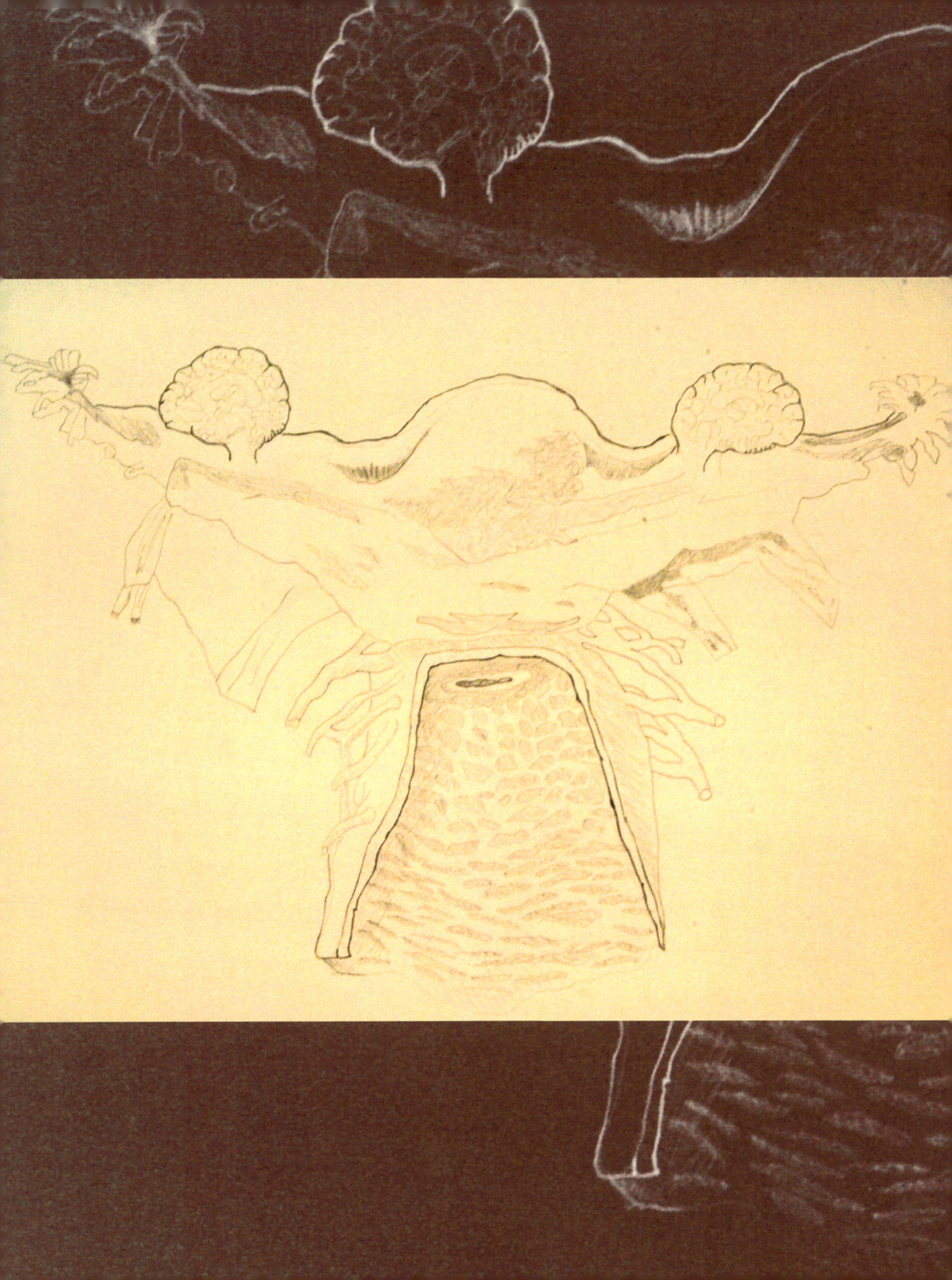

If time is linear, you just have to make sure that you aren't caught.

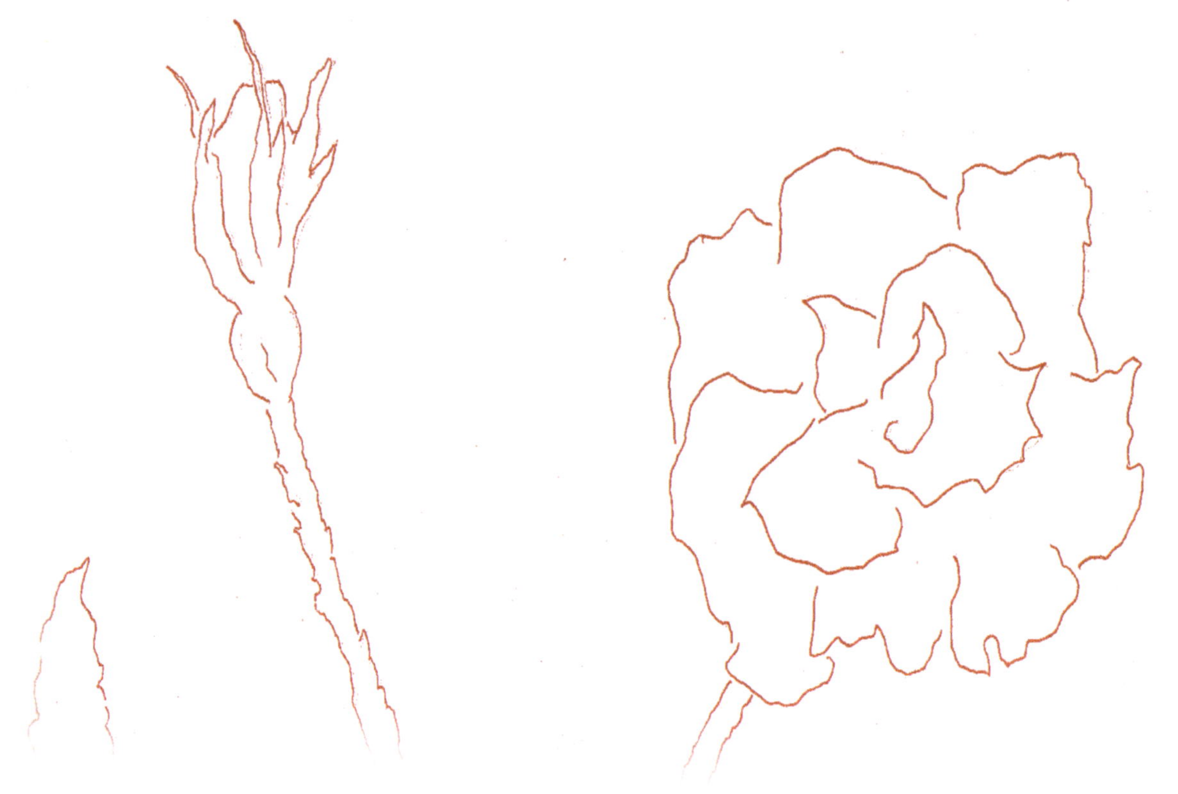

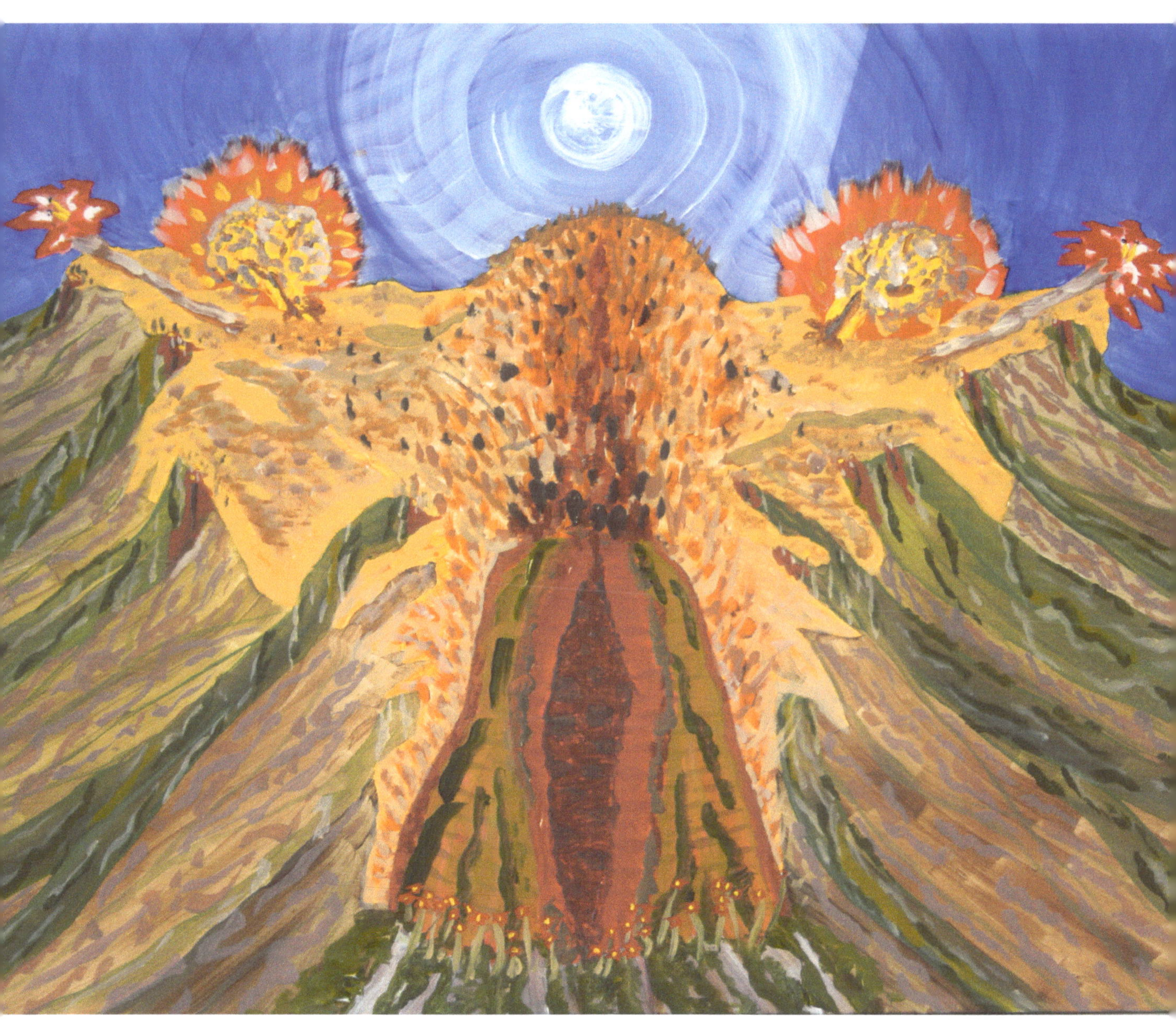

As I am not fluent in the languages of advanced physics,
I wouldn't be able to prove
the movement of time,
or even the structure of Space-Time,
is cyclical or otherwise.

I would say that everything else
seems to be measured
against the units of Time,
and that Time itself
feels like it is
a texture of consciousness
by which other textures are felt.

The moment I wake up in the morning
feels like a reawakening of consciousness.
Every moment could feel like this
if cyclical time was a given.

You feel things in the moment
by, with and against the moment of time
you remember them in.

Your awareness is located in time,
but chooses to split
up the huge circle into chunks

The arrival of the 07:25 train

is an agreed construct of minds,

As is the feeling of annoyance if it is late,

Or pleasure,

if you are as well.

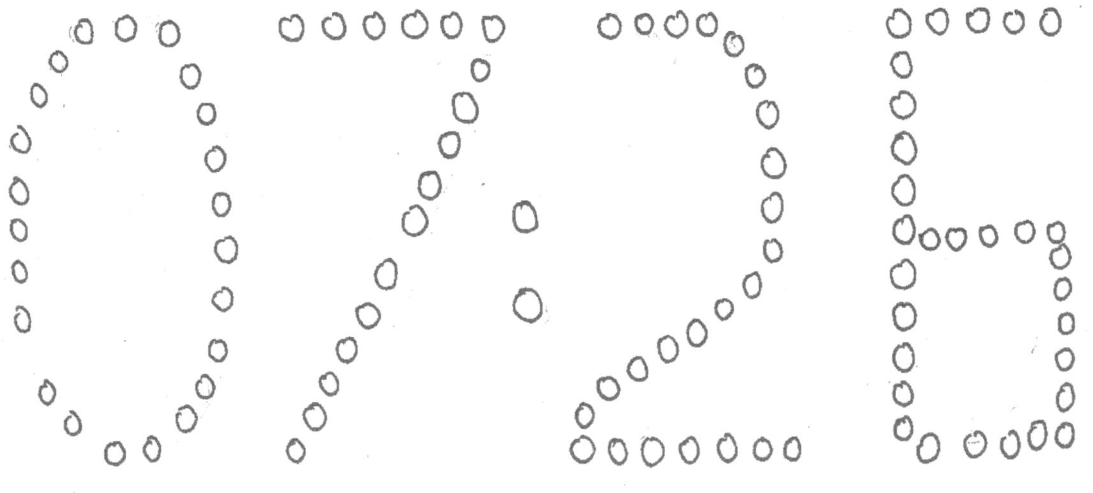

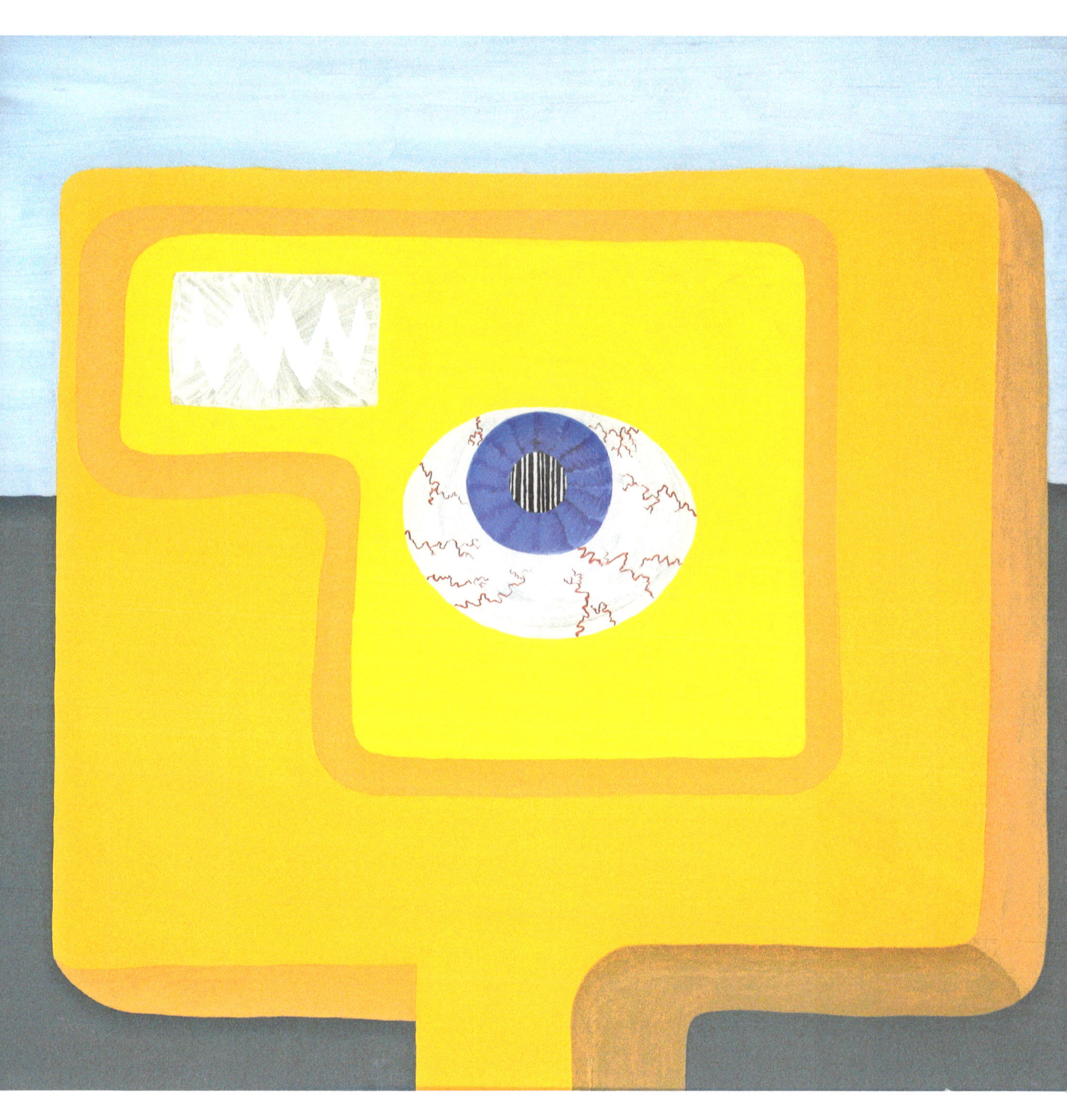

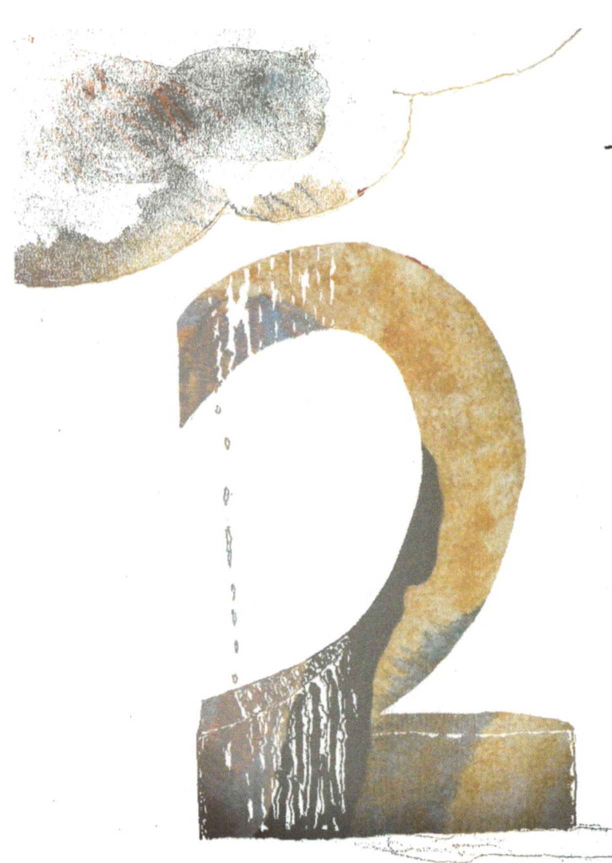

The use of Ritual as a Shamanic route to Realisation.

The process as Puja.

The feeling of water
yet even the process of washing dishes
or your hair.
Can be tiresome
If you want to
do something else.
However,
If you really
c o n c e n t r a t e
on the feeling of the activity,
It can have it's own
Ritualistic pleasure and purpose.
Mindful even.
The Essenes and Sadhus
Knew and Know about
Baptism without plumbing
From the Ganges to
the Jordan.

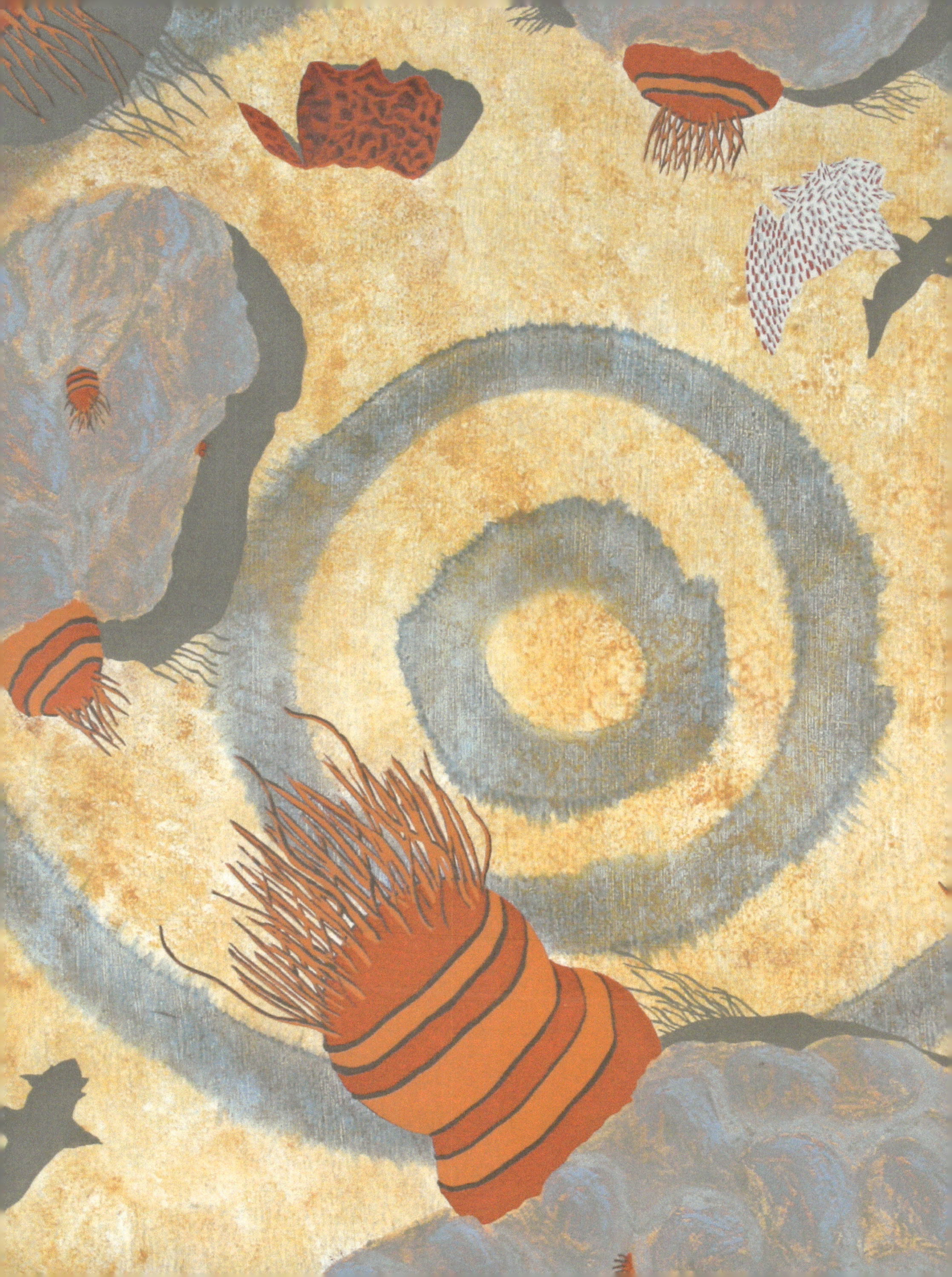

The Tantric concept of Puja is an interesting one.
- A routine activity that becomes ritualised
and therefore magical.
I have been painting for a long time,
both making art in the form of paintings
and decorating houses with filler, paint and wallpaper.

The more you do
the more the activity becomes ritualised,
from mixing colours on a palette,
to stirring a tin of undercoat.

This is how craft becomes art and vice versa.

Of course,
the language of drawing and painting
becomes a whole map of higher value meaning.
But that is as much about context
as anything else,
in the same way as a beautifully decorated room
is worth more money
when the room is in a smarter
part of town.

The action of applying liquid coatings
onto any surface
Is made with the same hands
and sometimes the same paint.

The ritual of both activities both occupy time
in the same way
and can put me in the same state of mind.
Both activities feel like a shamanic route to realisation.

In the studio you have the luxury of a self-directed brief,
you can make whatever you want,
someone else might want it,
but that's not why you are making it.
You are performing the ritual of
the realisation of your Self.

Whereas when you are on site you are
cleansing and transforming someone else's container.
The ritual is performed for the realisation
of the other -
The Self as other -
and some cash.

Any activity,
from raking gravel
to fixing a motorbike,
can raise your awareness.

Painting is my activity.

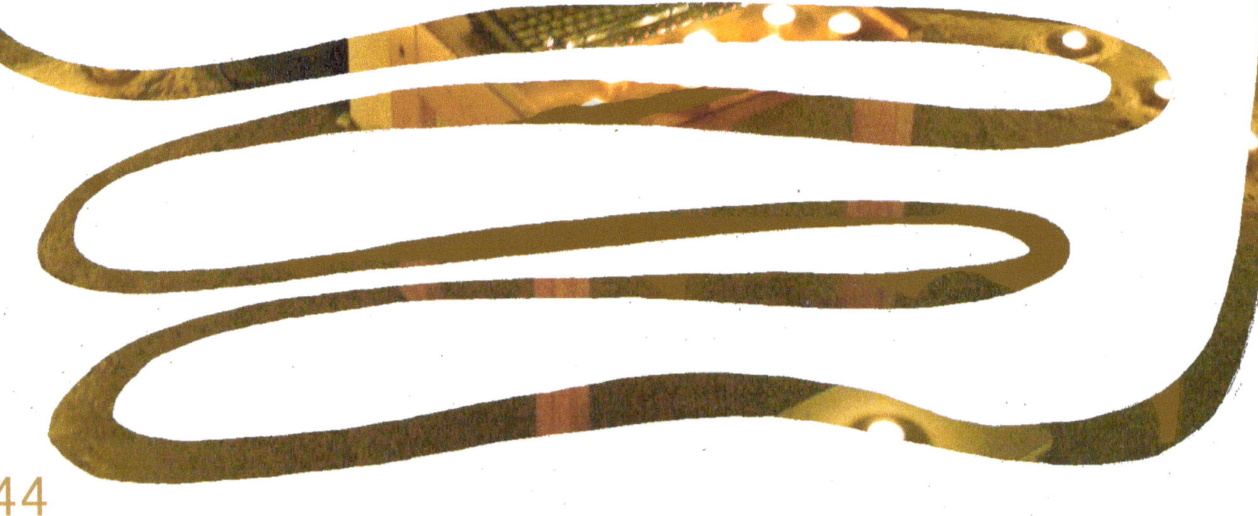

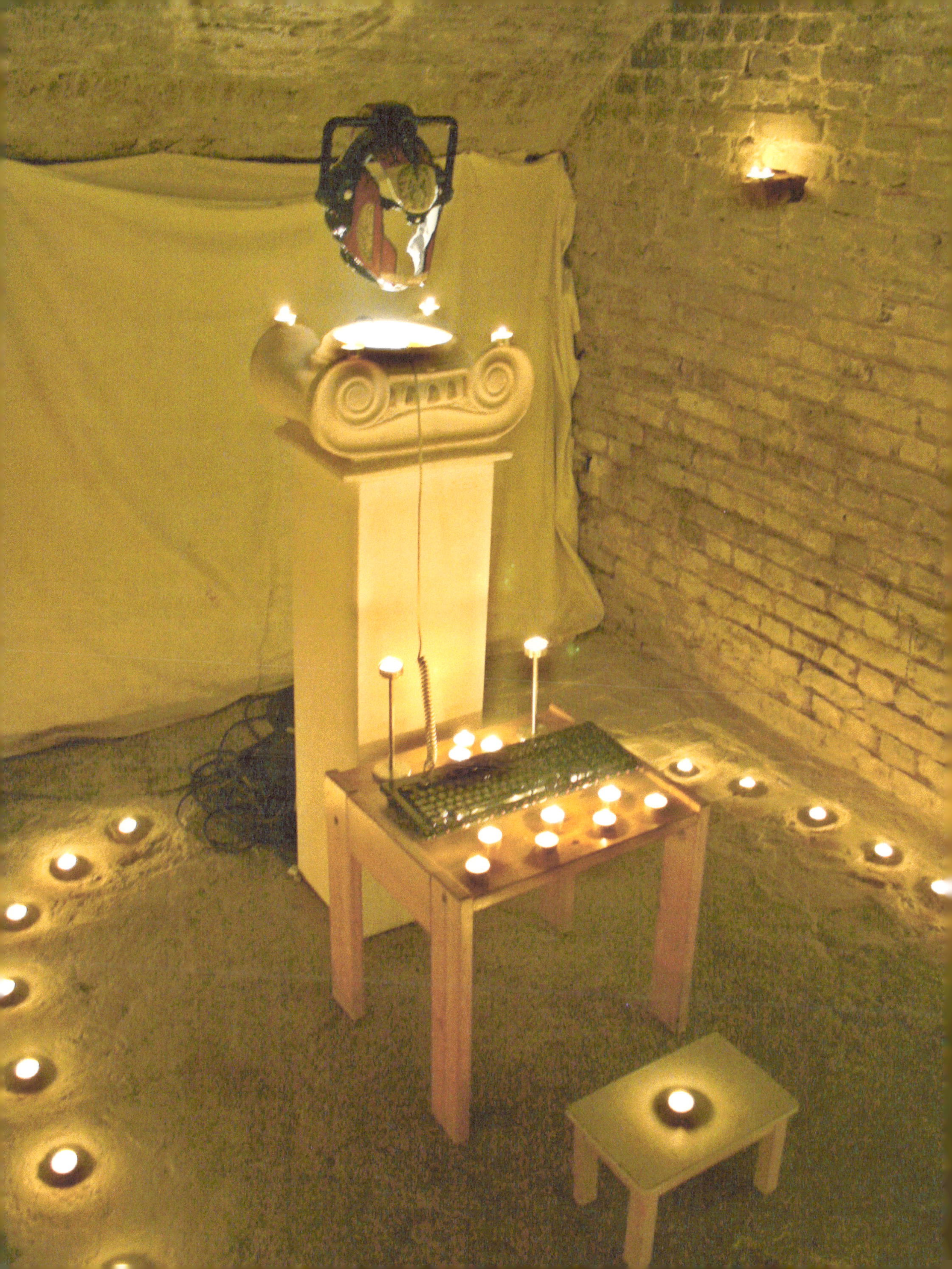

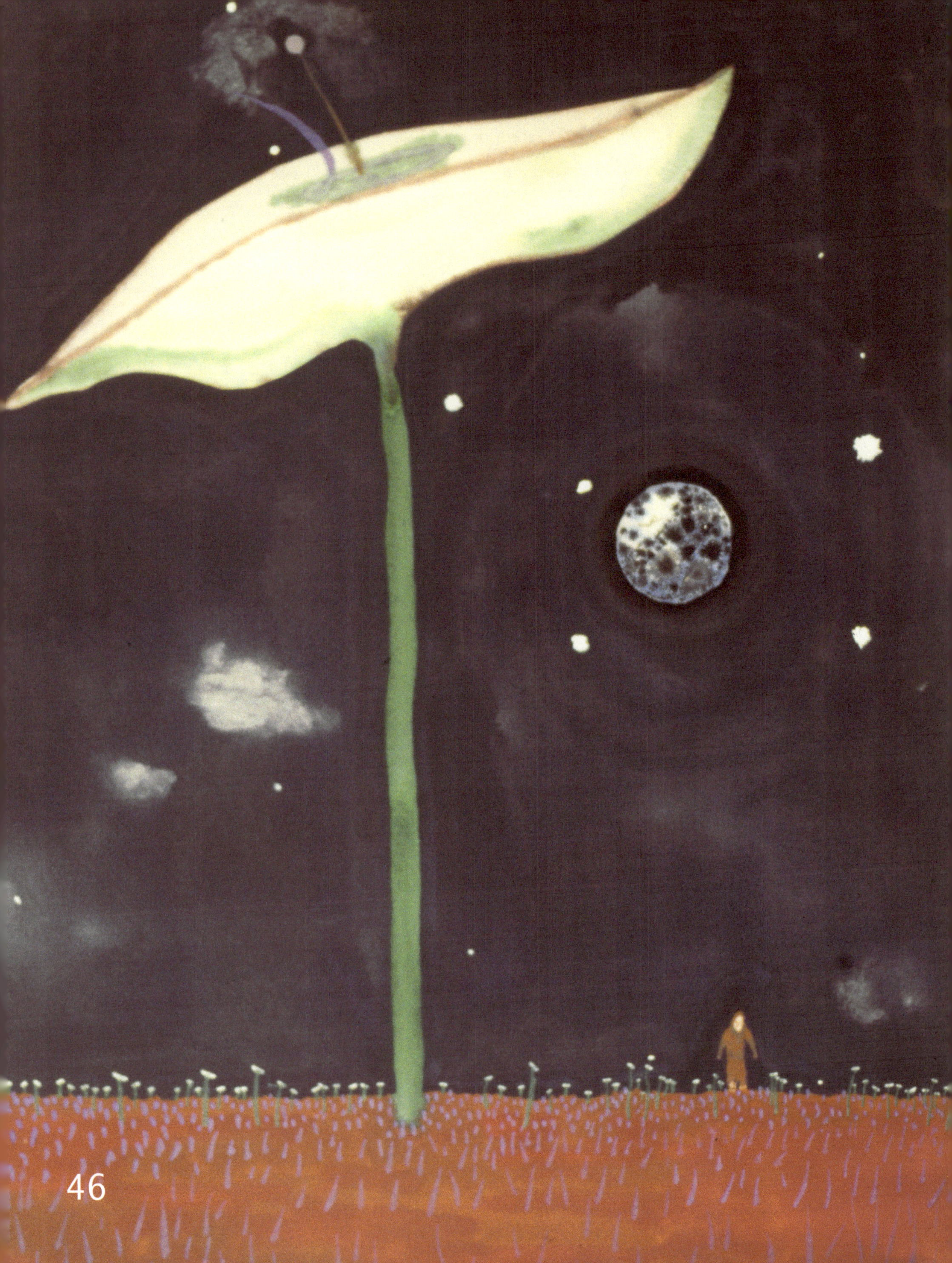

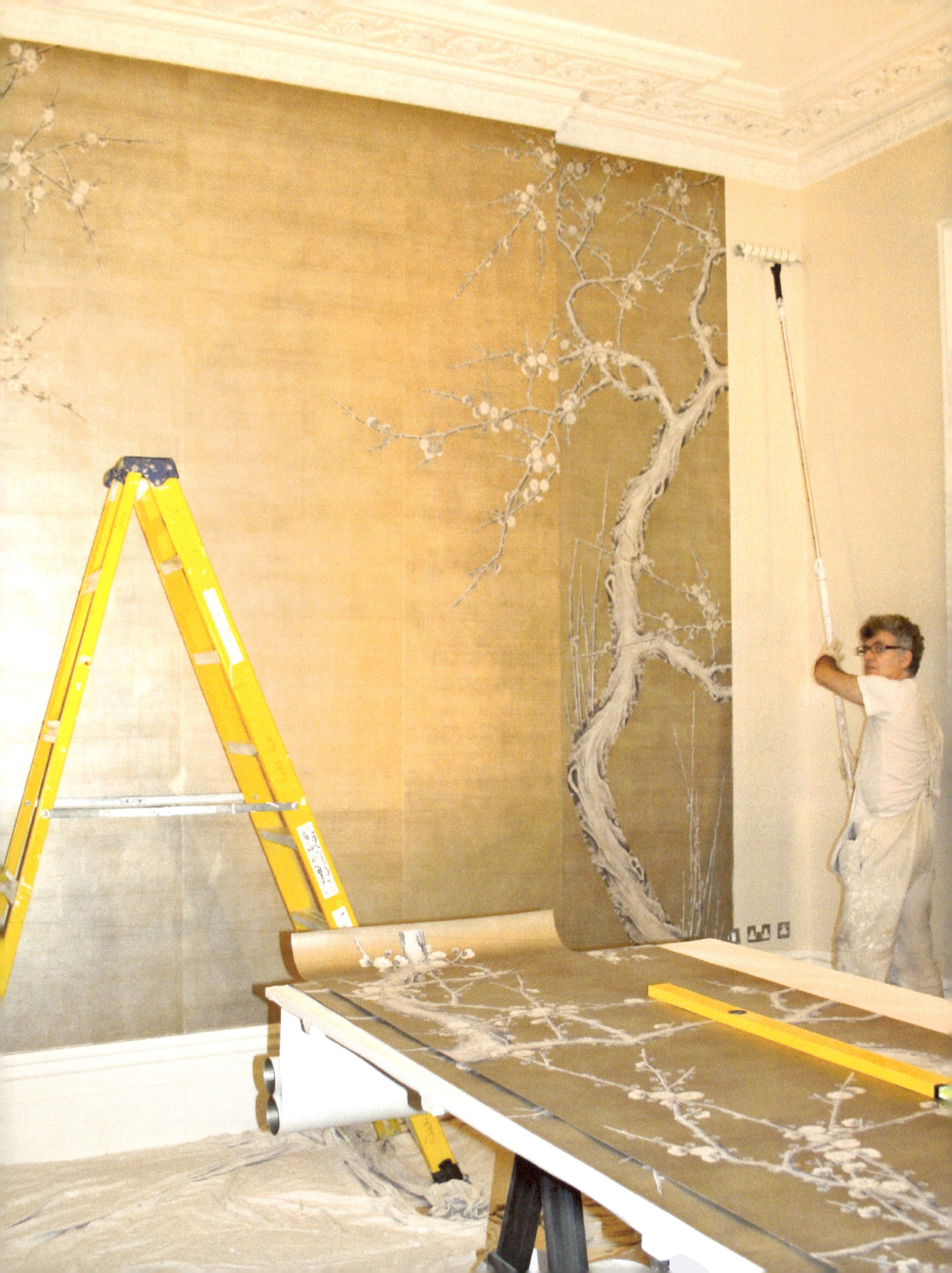

The Blank Space

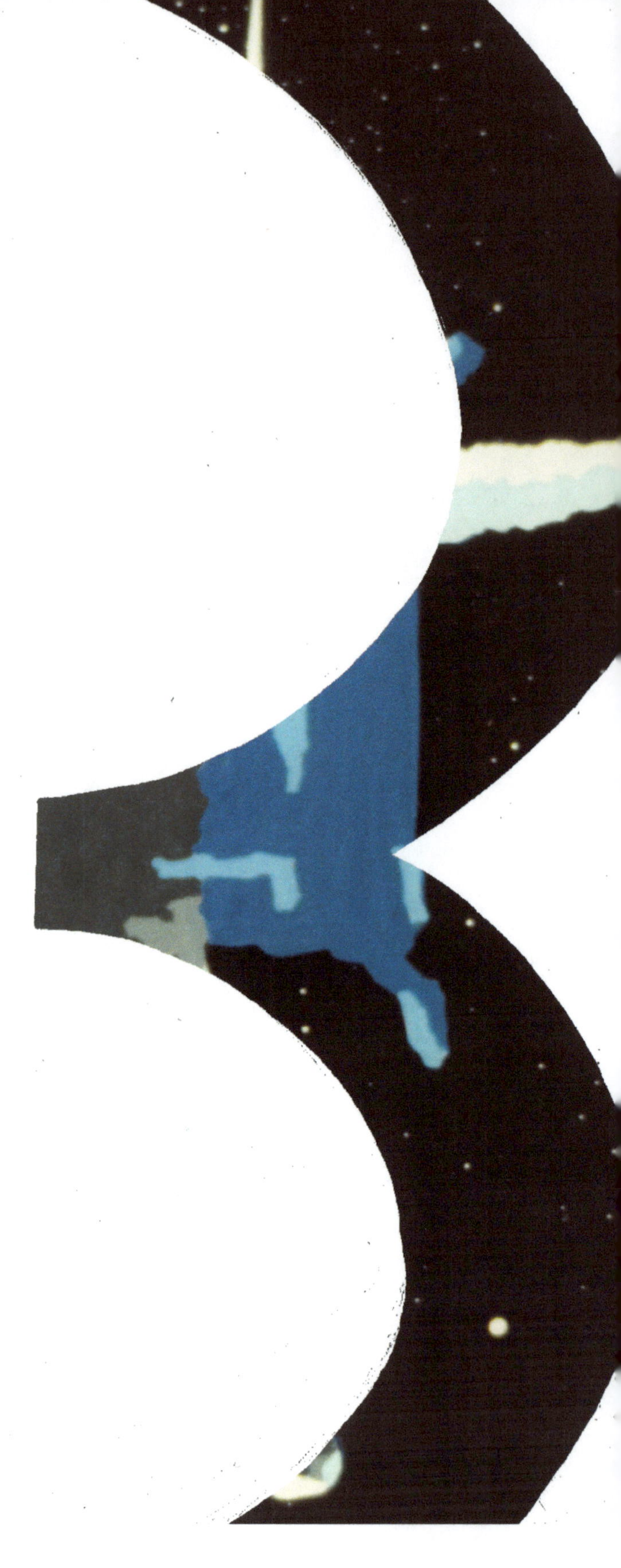

In the day-to-day human world,
which seems full of endless data and distraction,
the whole universe is very difficult
for one human mind to encompass.

Since most of the universe is empty space,
the meditative practice of emptying the mind
is ironically one route
to that emcompassing process.

In painting,
or writing for that matter,
the blank page can seem overwhelming,
as anything that you put down
isn't something else,
and maybe that something else
is what you are after,
not the thing you have just put down.

It is the crisis of creation
that is the 'block'.

Of course
you just need to get
stuck into the rituals

and come back
and make corrections later.

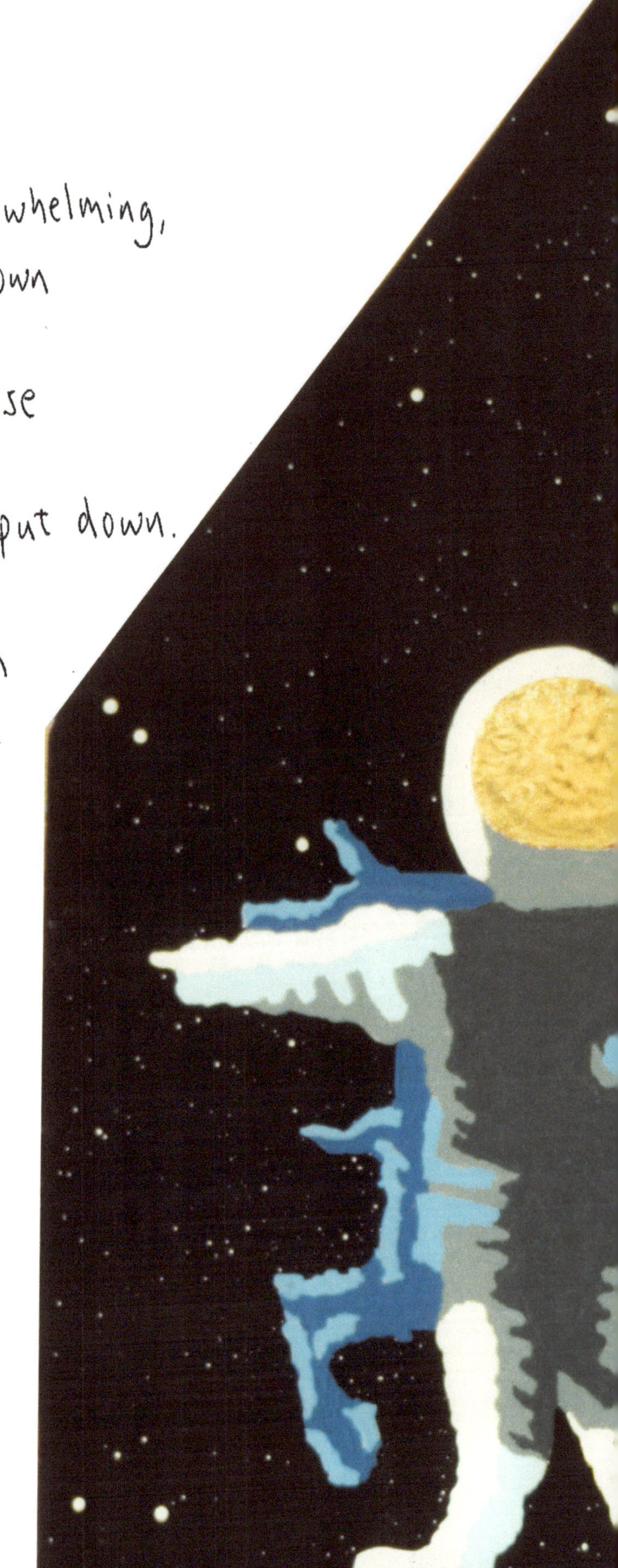

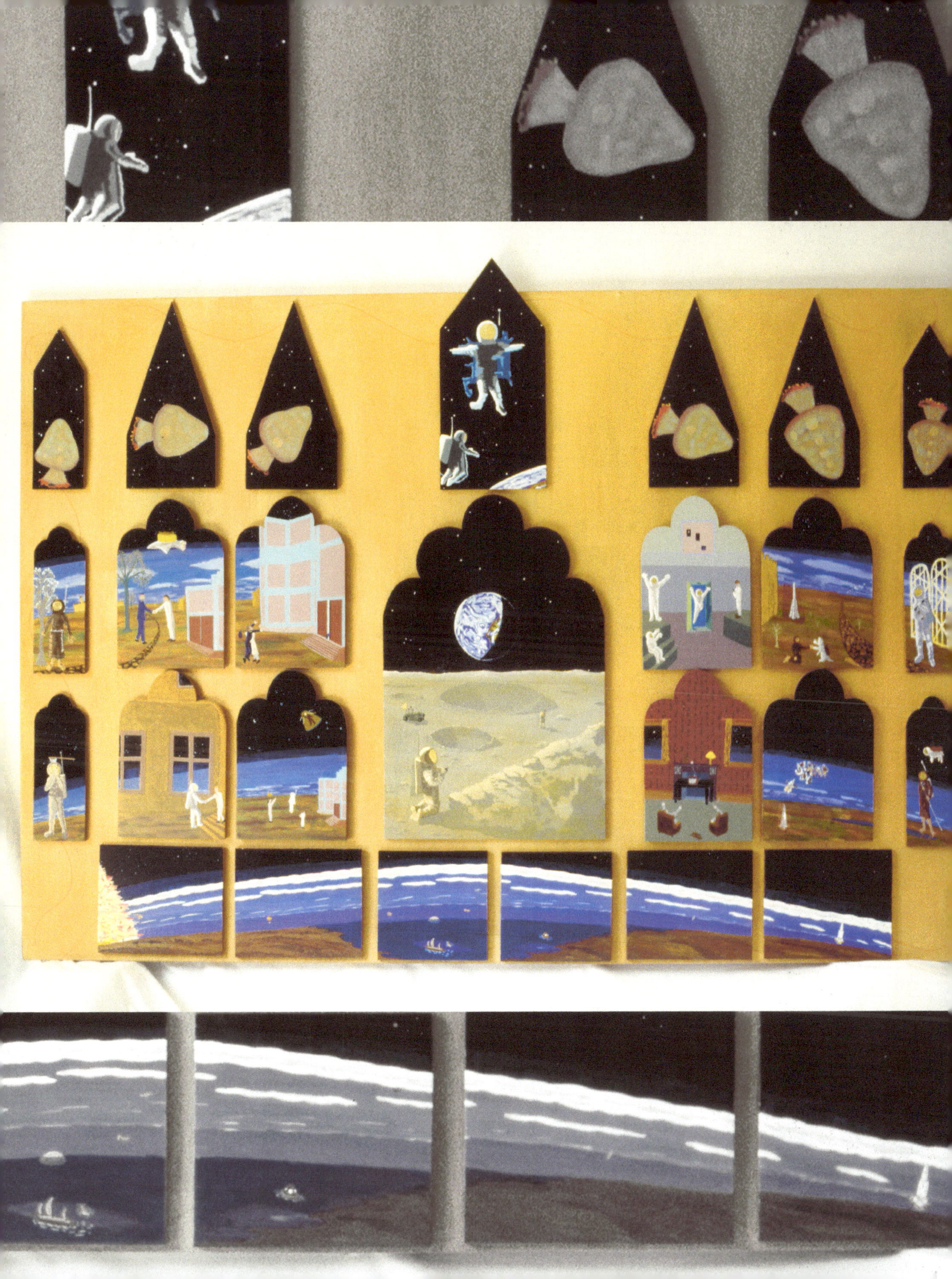

Intuition as a valid process.

Verbal and non-verbal.

Music and the play of time.

Map micro-macro brain-city

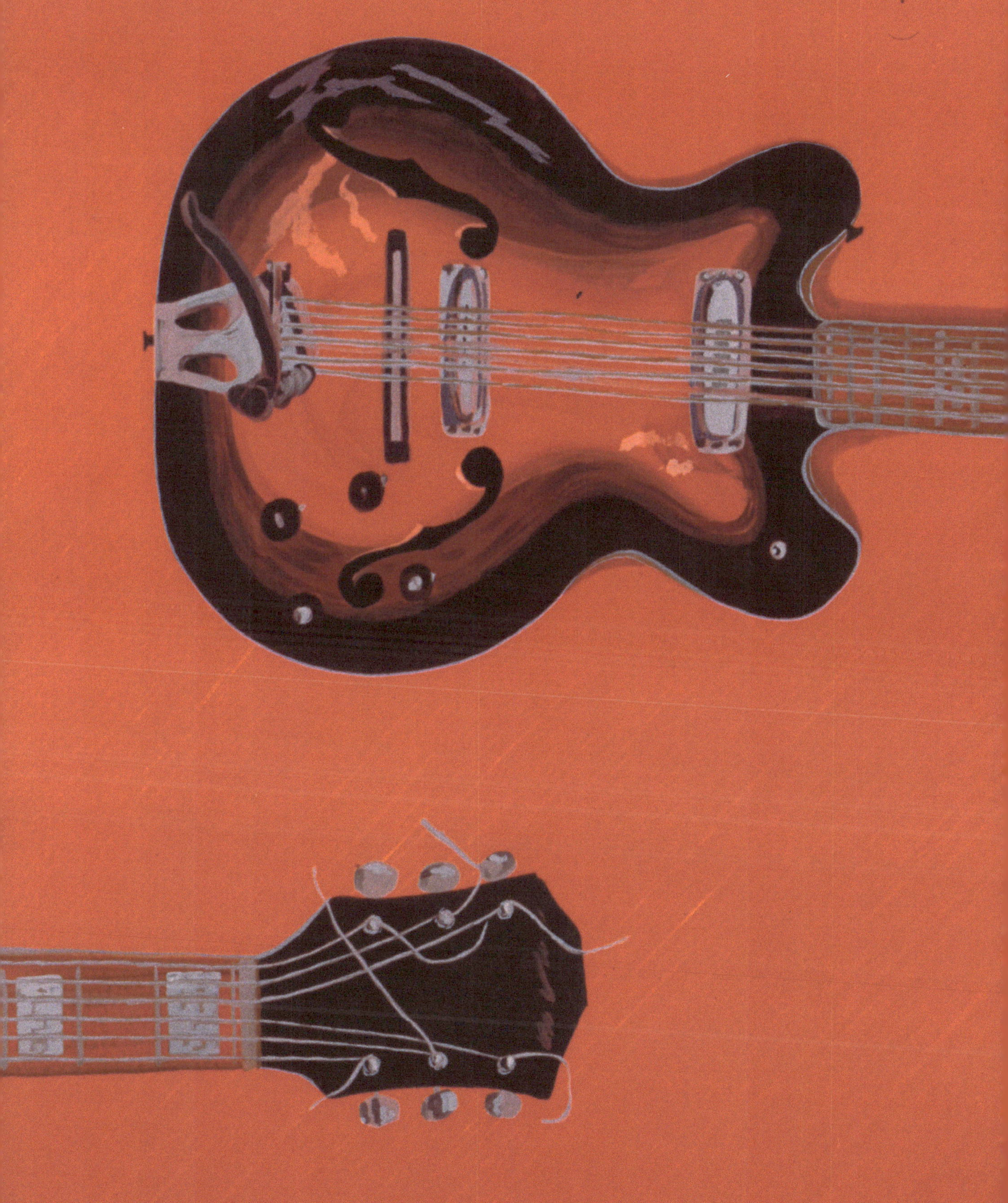

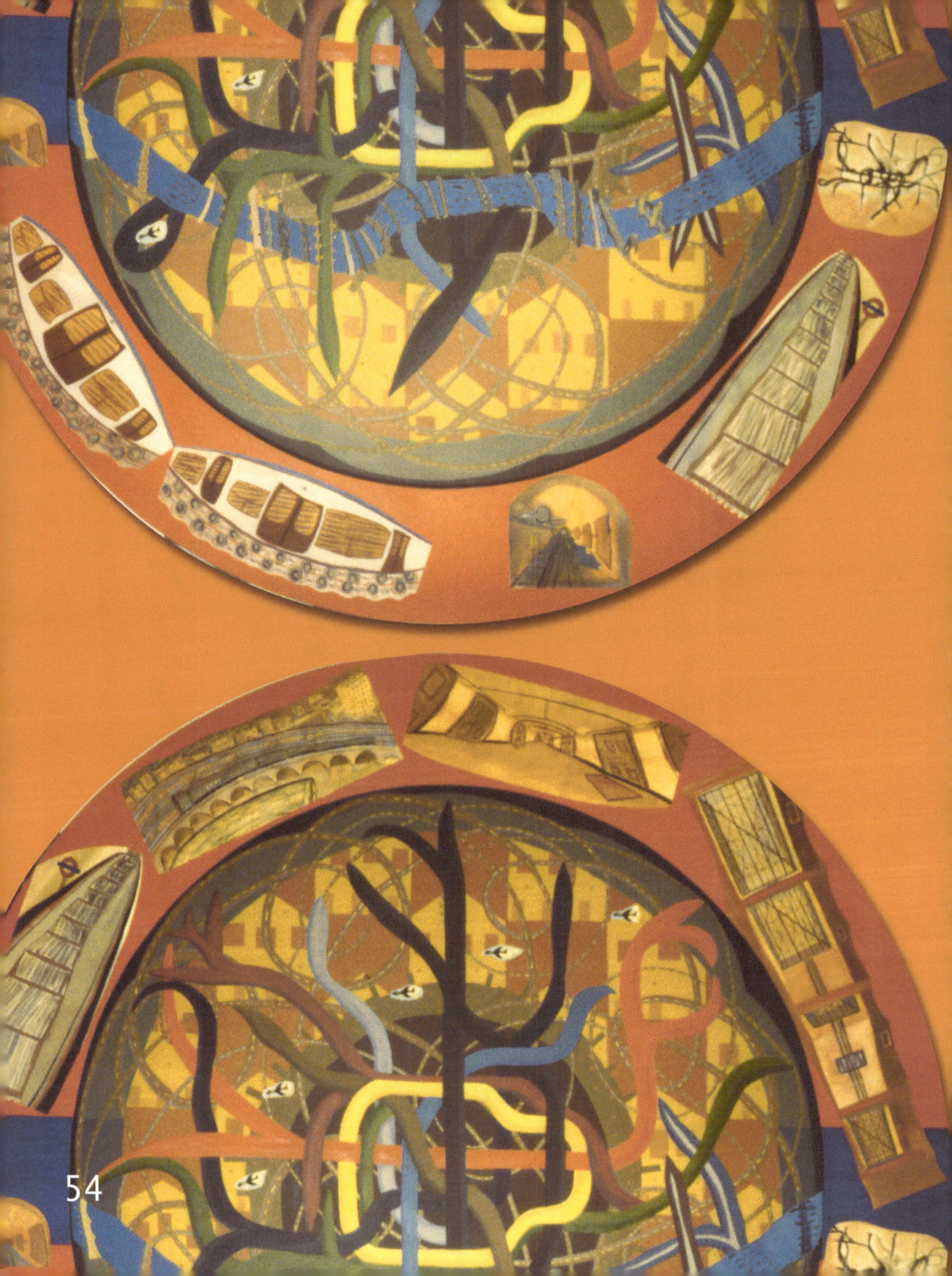

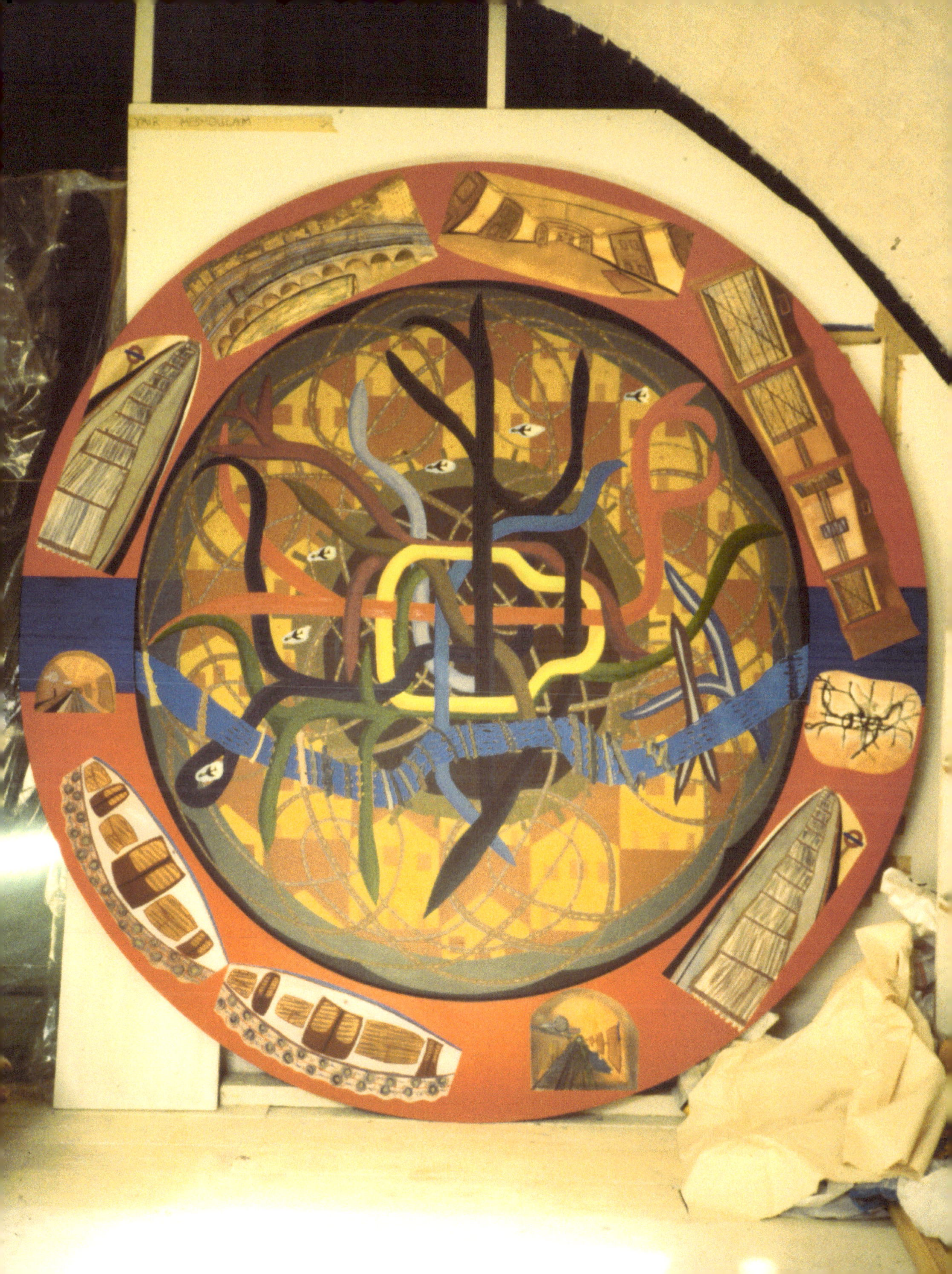

Maps are also superb diagrams of consciousness, where one thing is in relation to another
The human mind seems to make its own map out of experience, signs and memory.

The memories are stacked up with

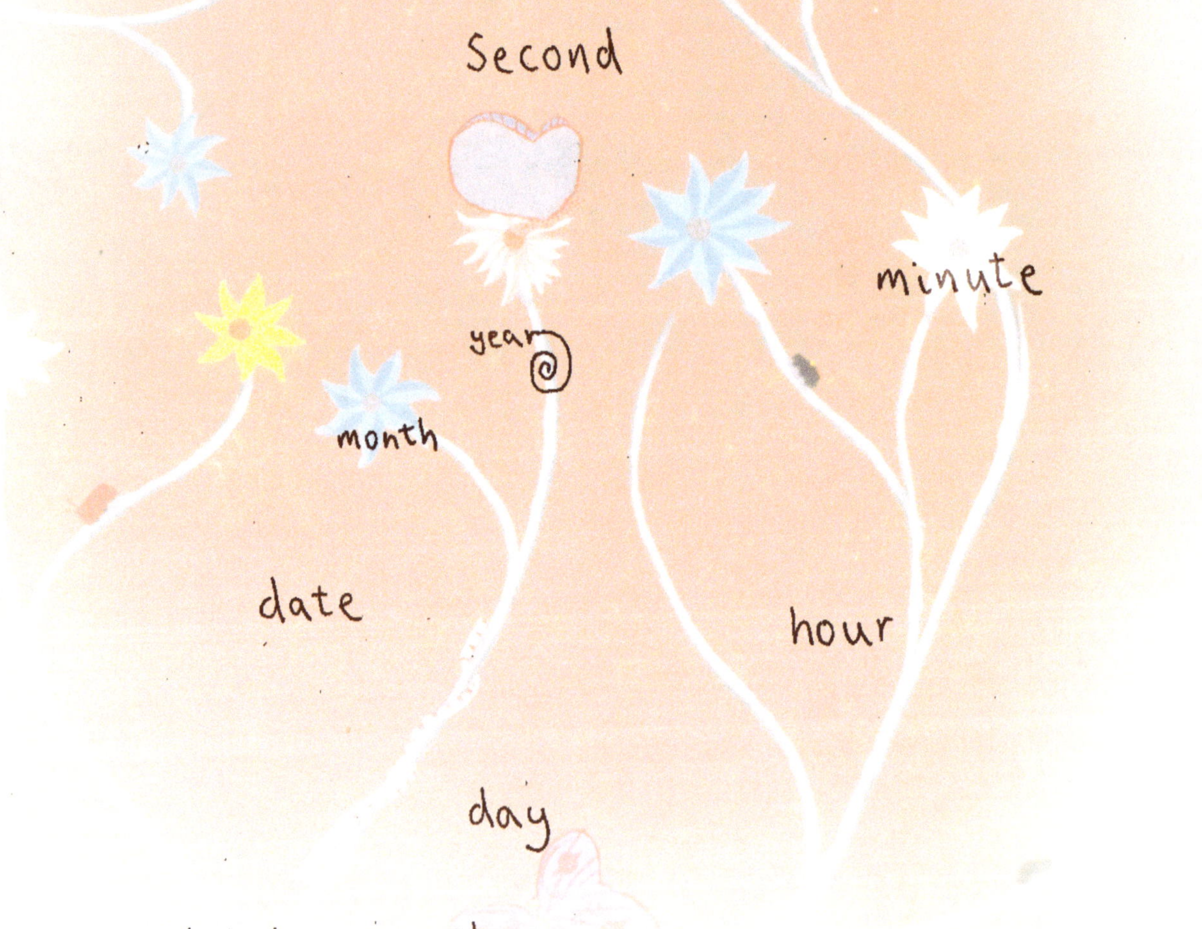

Second

year

minute

month

date

hour

day

time labels on them.

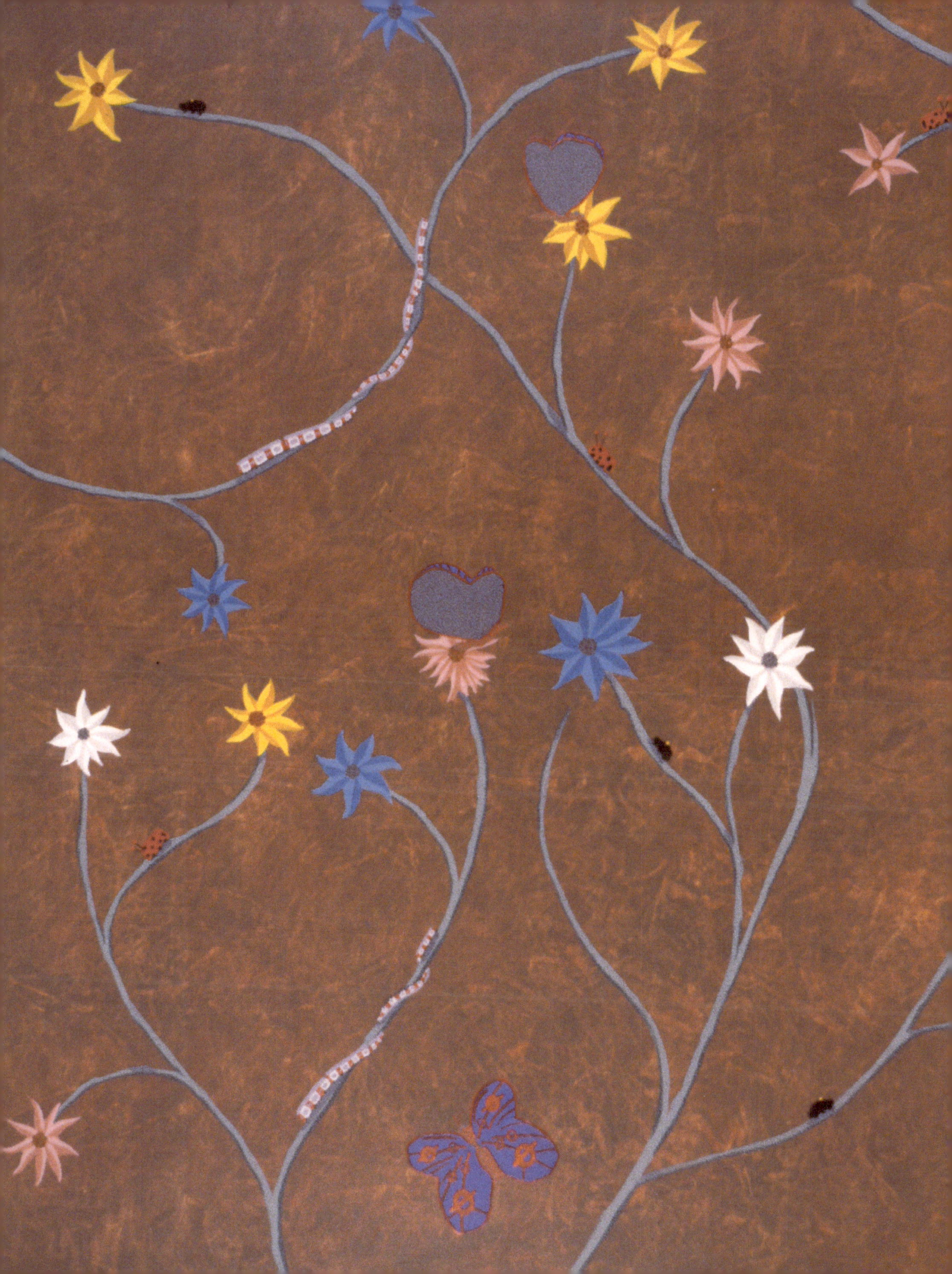

If you ignore

the difference

in scale,

there seem to be

remarkable similarities

remarkable similarities

between

the structure of things

on a

Small

and on a large scale.

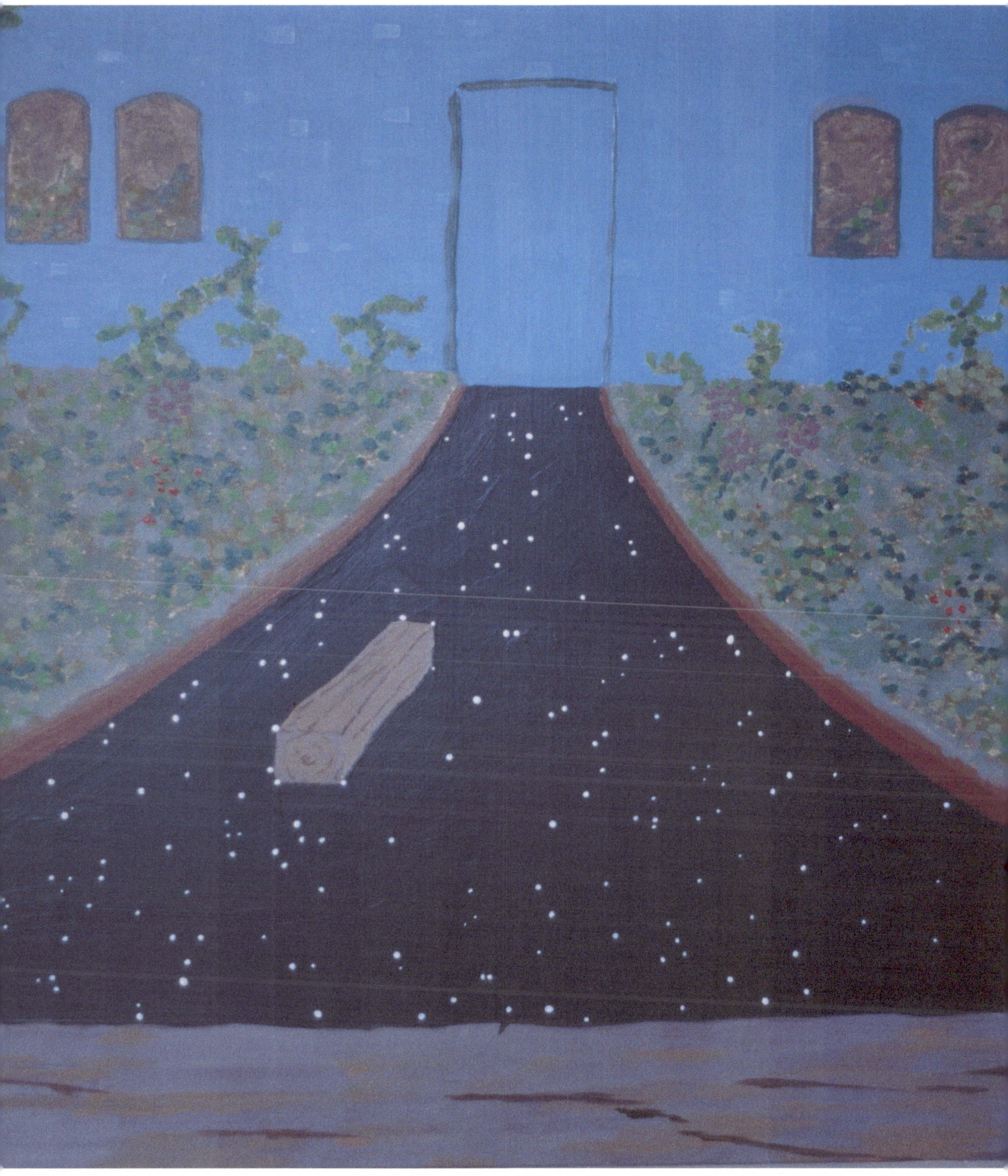

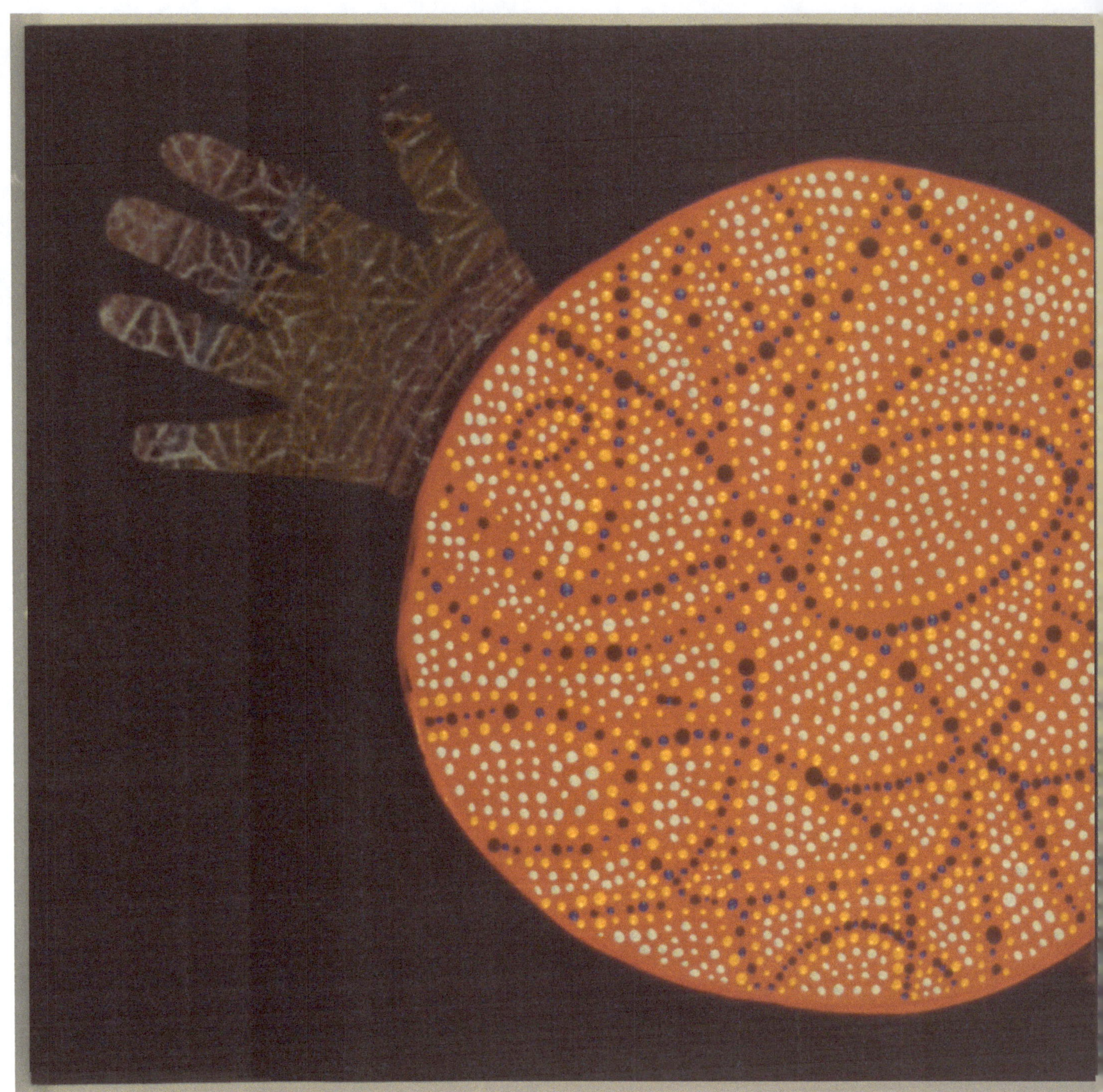

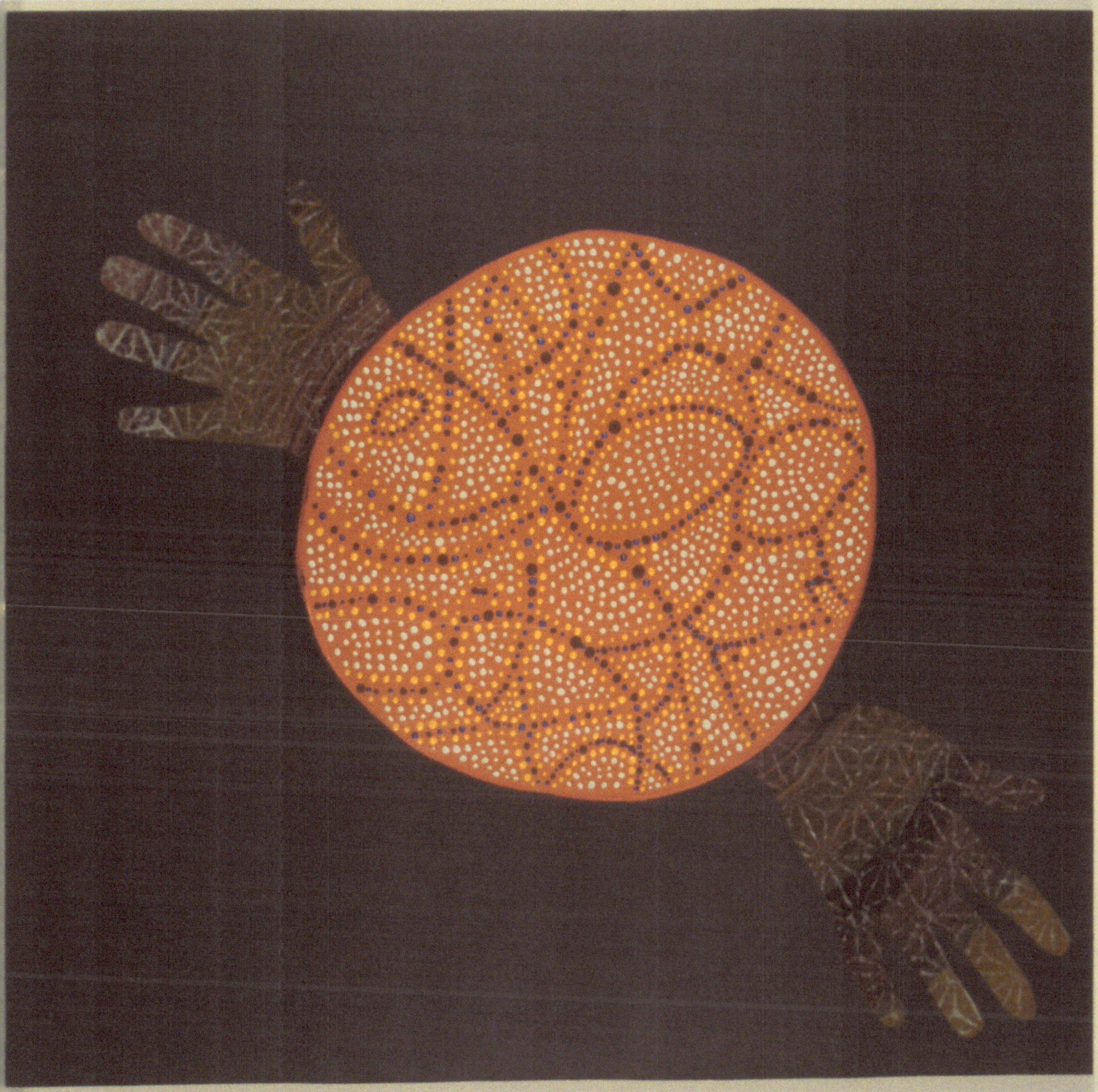

I think the brain
is like a city
and vice versa.

It may be that the structure
of one is replicated
in the other.

The Internet may also
be an expansion of the city,
and both form
an electrical network
of human consciousness.

I think the brain
is like a city
and vice versa.

It may be th
of one is replicated
in the other.

The Internet may
be an expan
and both form
an electrical network
of human conscious

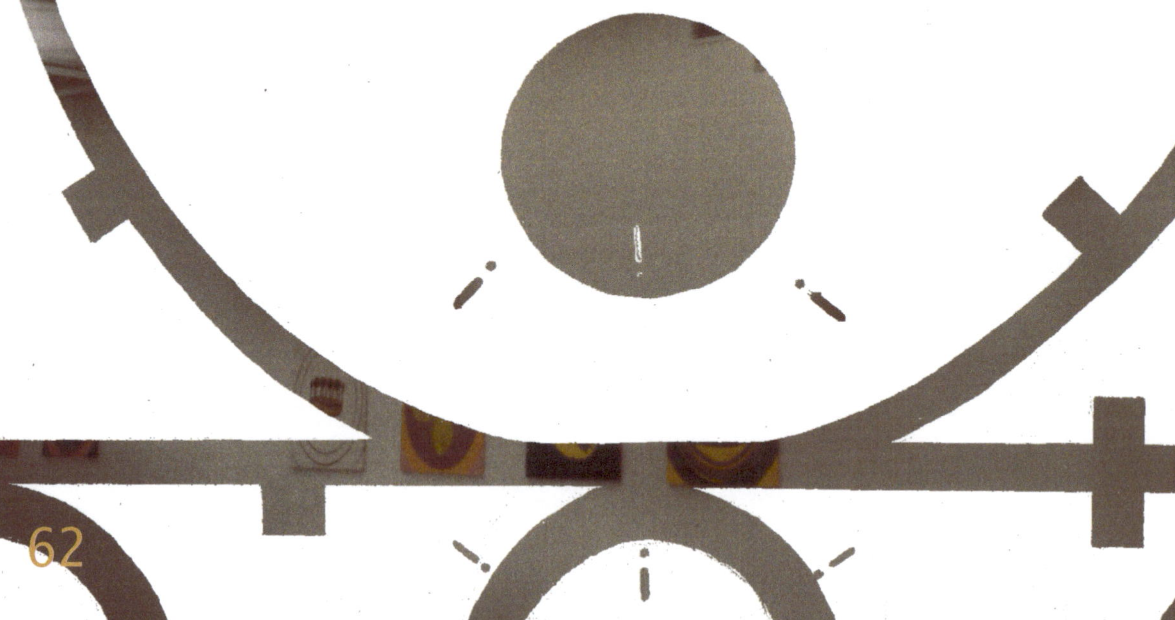

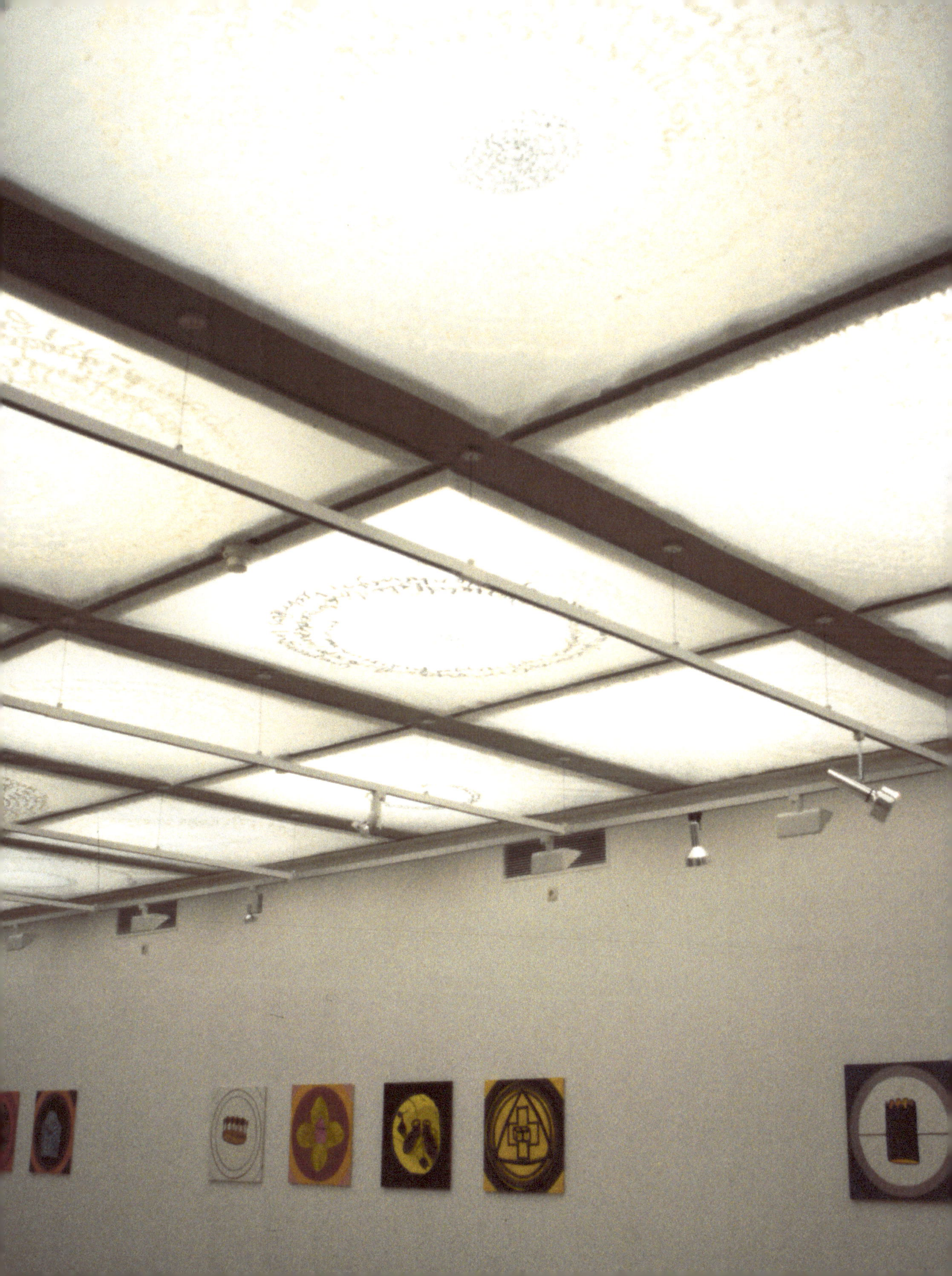

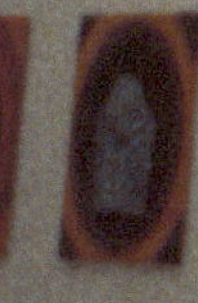
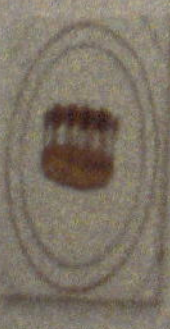
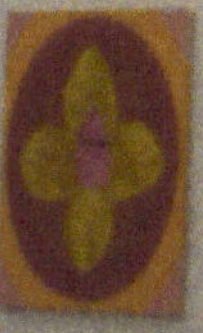
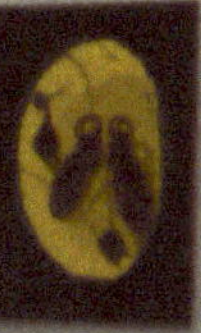
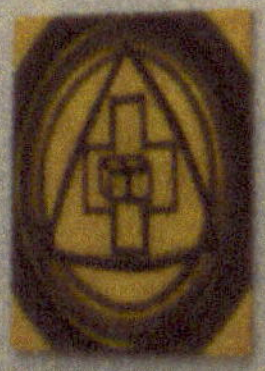
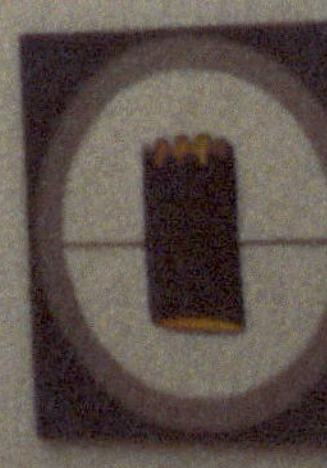

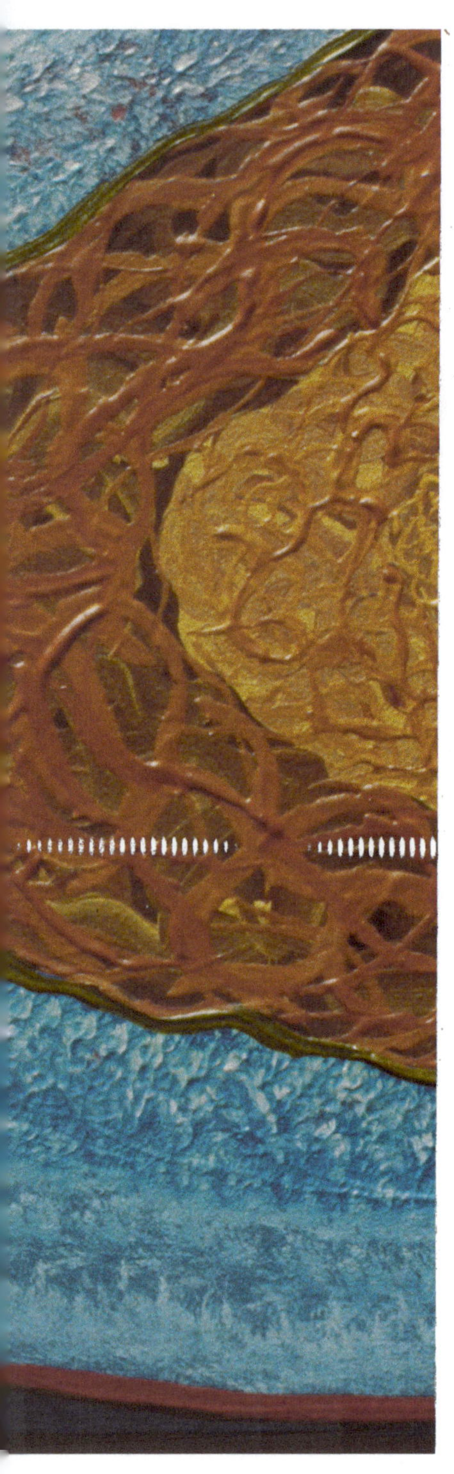

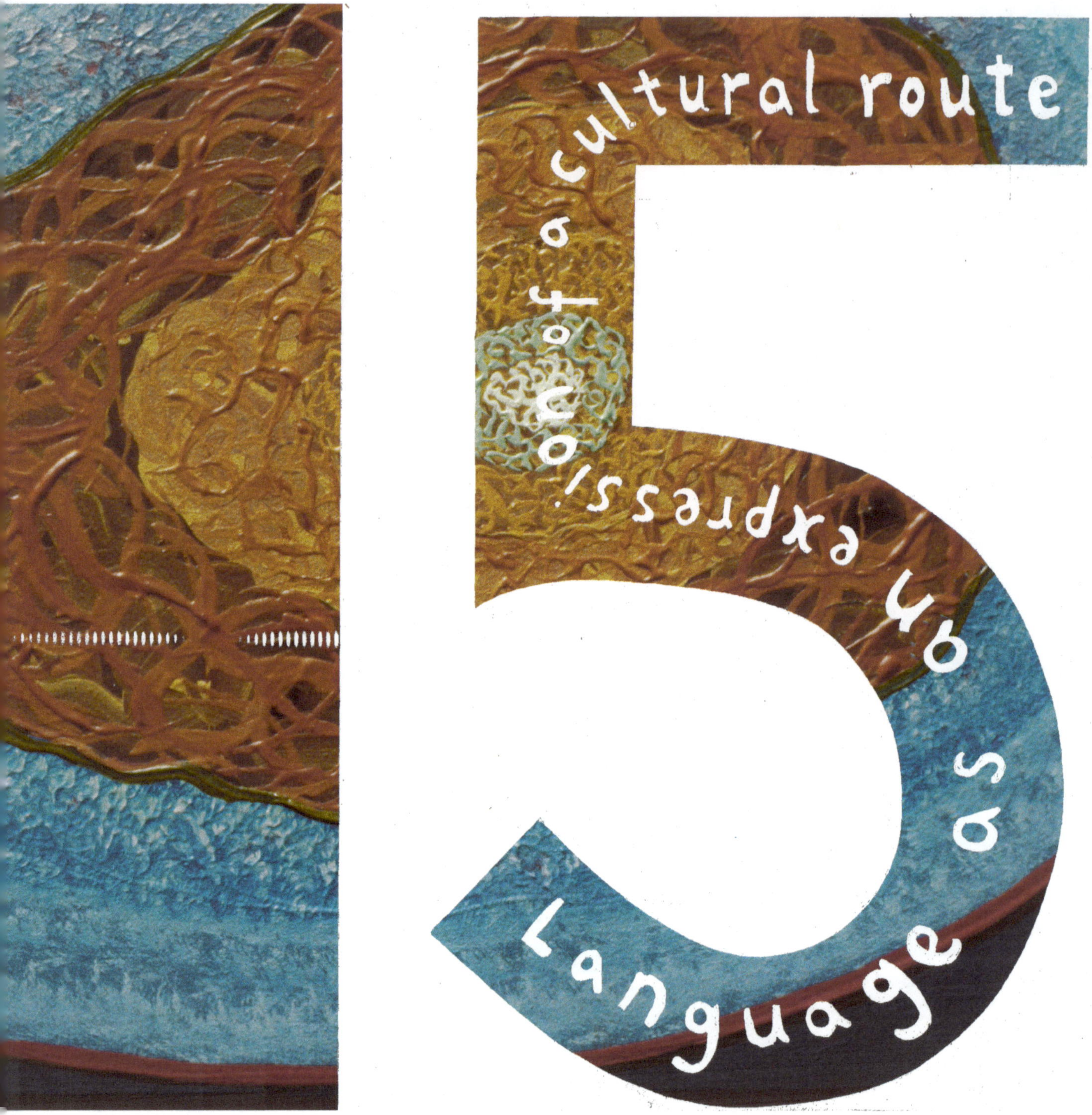

15 Language as an expression of a cultural route

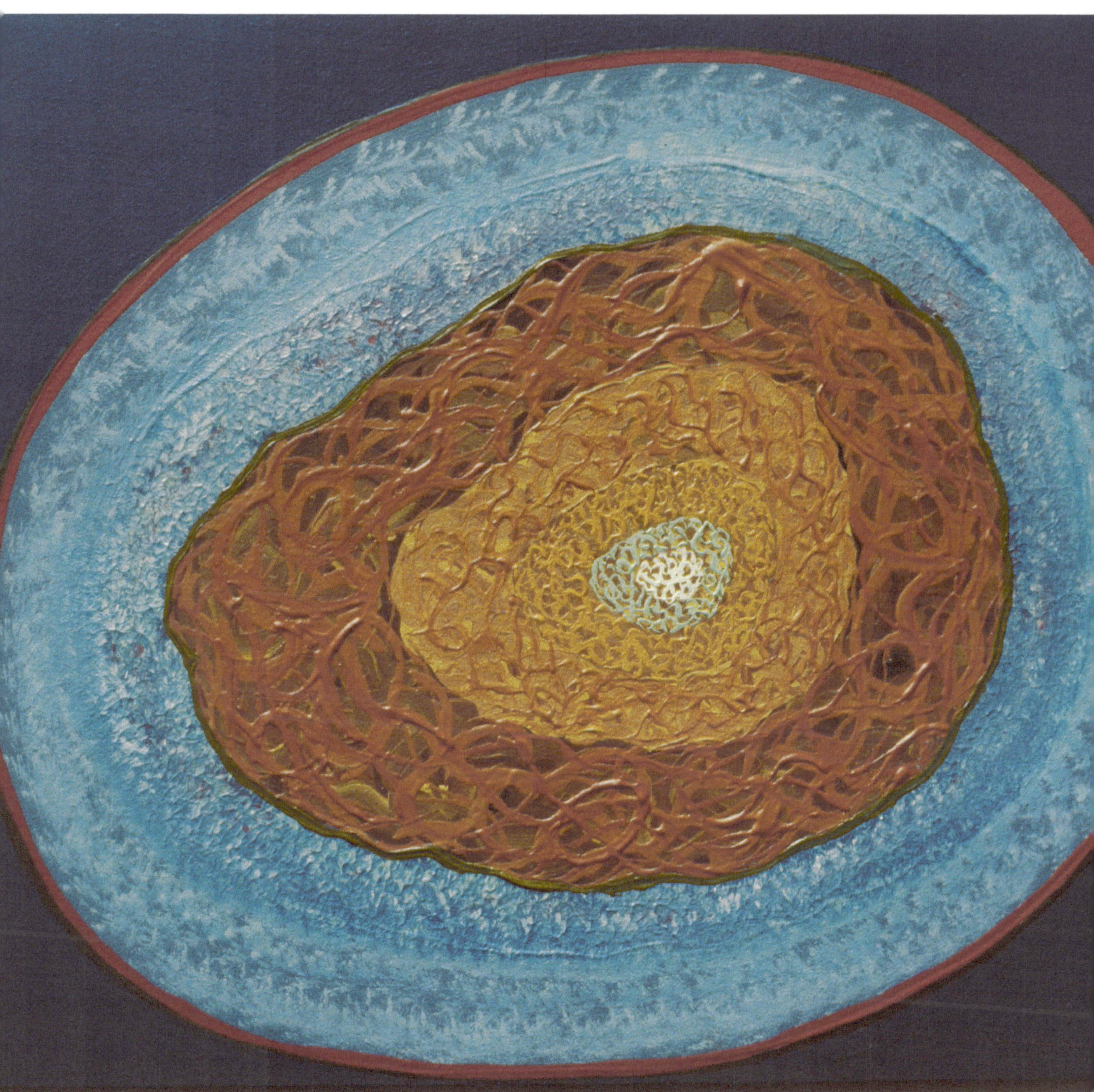

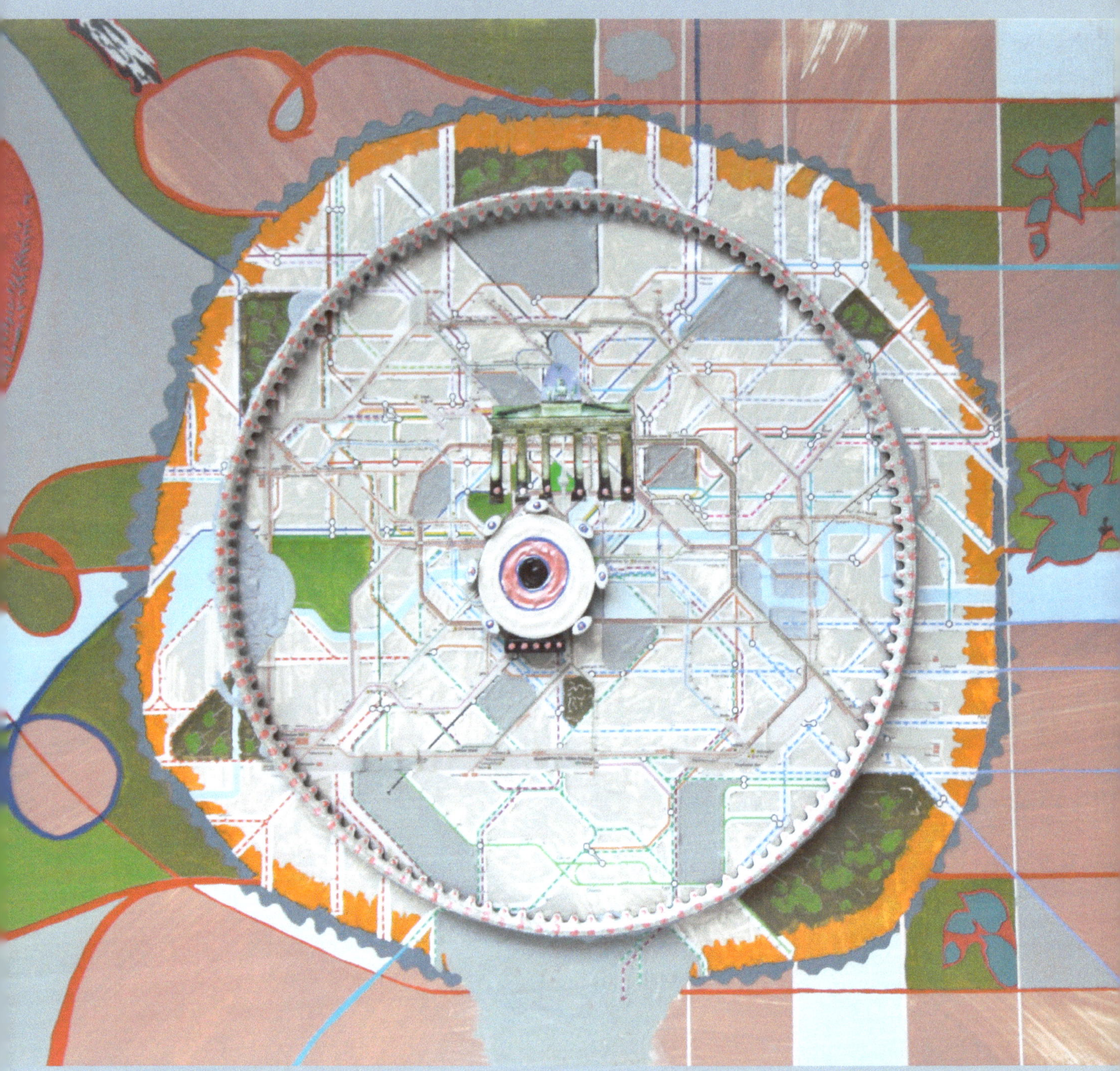

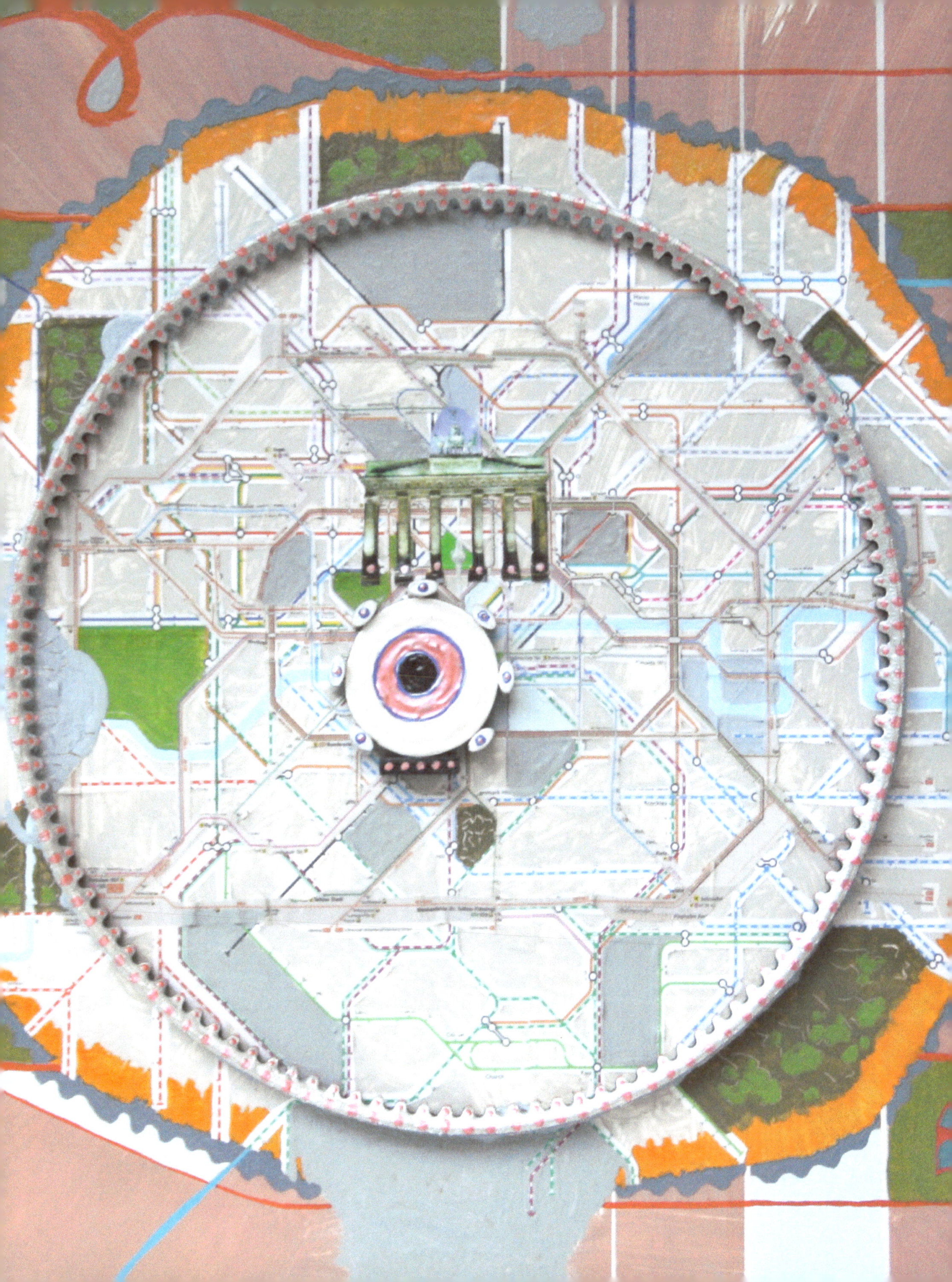

Confusing Conclusion

It has been
interesting to view
my work over the past
25 years in the light of this
most recent project, but difficult
to pin down exactly what
I have discovered.

Partly because whatever meaning there is
in the pictures,
or in the making of the pictures,
But mainly because non-verbal objects
can't be summed up neatly
in a text next door to them.

There are threads running through those discoveries,
probably cyclical ones,
and therefore ones I have discovered before,
and will discover
again.

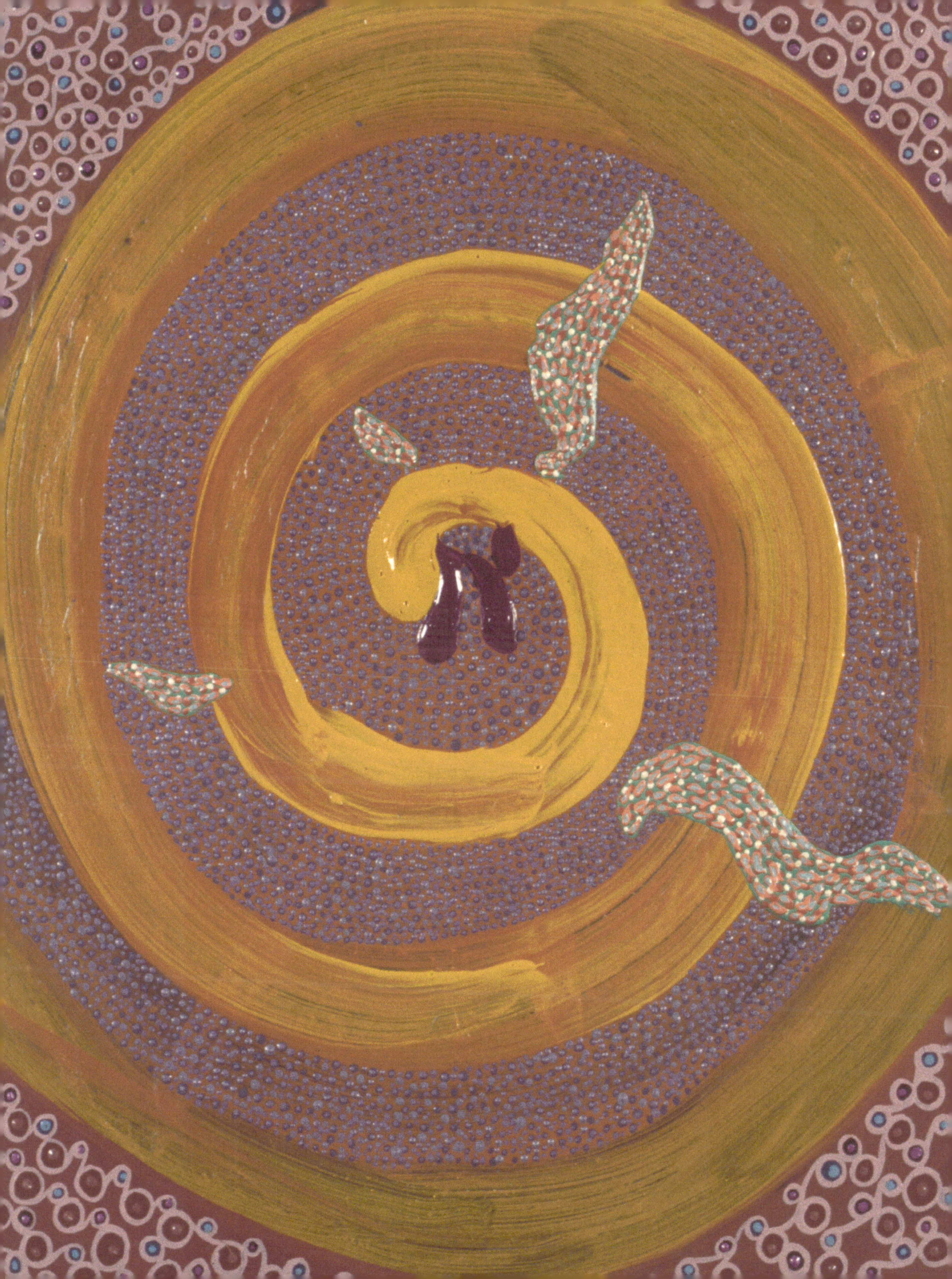

Contributions from Friends

Locked-in-Syndrome

by

Karl-Heinz Pantke

Linda Loschinski and Julia Szymetzko

1. Introduction

What is consciousness? Where is it? What is the texture of consciousness? How can one find out? The German philosopher Thomas Metzinger said that "the problem of consciousness builds – together with the question of how the universe is formed – the furthermost borderline of the humans` pursuit of knowledge." [1]

Every scientific discipline is trying to locate and define the phenomenon of consciousness in its own way. Hundreds of years ago, the philosopher John Locke defined the human mind as a blank sheet of paper, a "tabula rasa" on which experience writes our story. In this way of thinking, perception is – so to speak – the beginning of awareness. [2]

Of course – over the centuries – consciousness became a profound matter of interest in every discipline even beyond philosophy and it is still closely observed and controversially discussed. Today there are several meanings of consciousness: it can be an equivalent to subjectivity or to awareness but it is also defined as the ability to feel or experience. In neuroscience there even exists the theory of consciousness being purely physical. [3]

In the 19th century neuroscientists started to look for consciousness in the brain and its structure. [4] Is it possible that the texture of consciousness is of physical nature? Or is it the way we construct our consciousness in our daily narrations? When we live to see something, we try to communicate our emotions and experiences to others. That is one way to construct our identity.

1 Metzinger, T. (1995): Bewusstsein. Beiträge aus der Gegenwartsphilosophie. [Consciousness. Contributions from temporary philosophy.] Ed. Metzinger. Mentis: Paderborn, p. 1.

2 See also Locke, J. (2001): An essay concerning human understanding. Batoche: Kitchener.

3 See also Prinz, J.J. (2012): Could Consciousness be Physical? The Brain Maintained. Oxford University Press: Oxford. Chapter 10 and Tononi, G. (2004) An information integration theory of consciousness. In: BMC Neuroscience 5/ 2004. Issue 42.

4 See also Welsh, C. (2007): Die „Dunkelheit hinter dem Stirnportal". Begegnungen von Literatur und Hirnforschung zwischen 1800 und 2000. [The „Darkness behind our fronthead". Encounters between literature and brain research between 1800-2000.] In: Jahrbuch für Literatur und Medizin, vol. 1, p. 95-111.

But what if this isn't possible anymore? Consciousness can for example expand the understanding of another person talking about what he or she experiences/feels/notices. Yet how do we talk about what we are conscious of? Since Immanuel Kant it is known that consciousness is closely connected to subjectivity. So can one ever be sure about experiencing one object in the same way as another person? Can we be certain about experiencing the existence of the same tree as others? Do they see it, touch it, lick it, smell it, hear it as we do? And what about the consciousness of individuals who are not able to use all their senses? How do people feel whose senses are deprived feel? What is the texture of their consciousness?

People who suffer from the Locked-in-Syndrome[5] have a whole different way of experiencing the world. They are deprived, or find a change, of most of their senses. In autobiographical texts of patients suffering from Locked-in-Syndrome, their selfhood is often described as deconstructed mainly because of the missing possibility to communicate with their environment. The text "The diving bell and the butterfly"[6] by Jean-Dominique Bauby, who suffered a Locked-in-Syndrome, constructs a scene where the narrator is being trapped in the diving bell with just one eye as the "only link to the outside world".[7] He uses his mind to escape that horrible fate that this state represents for him.

It is known from clinical observation that often in such a state hallucinations take place. The brain tries to balance the missing proprioceptive information[8] and the borderlines between reality, dream and hallucination vanish in a totally paralyzed body. Both aspects can be seen in patients` reports. Günter Müller describes it in "In the Empire of hallucinations" (see chapter 6.2). Another good example can be found in "The diving bell and the butterfly". In the chapter "the alphabet" the narrator finds himself in a bed with letters dancing around him. He never explains the character of these pictures – he does not inform the reader whether he dreams or hallucinates it.[9] Finding a way to make this consciousness – with or without hallucinations – visible through speaking, writing, moving or spelling means hope for the patients suffering from diseases that deprive their senses.[10]

5 See also Laureys, S.; Pellas, F.; Eeckhout Van, P.; Ghorbel, S.; Schnakers, C.; Perrin, F.; Berré, J.; Faymonville, M.-E.; Pantke, K.-H.; Damas, F.; Lamy, M.; Moonen, G. and S. Goldman (2005): The Locked-in-Syndrome: What is it like to be conscious but paralyzed and voiceless? Prog Brain Res. 2005. Issue 150, pp. 495-511.

6 Bauby, J.-D. (1998): The diving bell and the butterfly. Vintage Books: New York.

7 ibid, p. 53.

8 See also Sacks, O. (2013): Hallucinations. Vintage Books: New York. 2013, chapter 2.

9 See also Bauby: The diving bell and the butterfly, p. 19.

10 See also Pistorius, M. (2011): Ghost boy. Simon&Schuster: London, p. xiii.

However suffering from Locked-in-Syndrome is not the only situation where people experience sensory deprivation. Where else does one experience that? This article tries to find an answer as to how consciousness is constructed and expressed if senses are deprived. Is it a horrible fate to have consciousness left as a tool of survival, a torture or just "part of the job"?

2. What is it that we call sensory deprivation?

2.1 Definition and history

Sensory deprivation is a method to alter human perception. Perception is a phenomenon experienced through the senses. Nearly every sense can be deprived for example by hoods or head masks (vision), earmuffs (hearing), a tank full of warm water (proprioception, orientation, thermoception) or gloves (touch). When senses are deprived or altered e.g. through monotony, the brain starts to produce alternative information and the result of this can be anxiety, panic, hallucinations or even psychotic episodes.

Already in the 1950s and 60s when the so called isolation tank was invented (see chapter 4), sensory deprivation has been a topic of experimentation. Many volunteers had the experience of having their senses deprived. All of them reported panic, anxiety or hallucinations. However, it also became a concept for a better understanding of our mind. Suddenly phenomena like the "gray-out" of pilots flying monotonously for hours without seeing the horizon, became understandable.

Sensory deprivation is not only a practice of modern times. Already in ancient times and during the 13th century, savants wanted to know more about human language and raised children in dark rooms without any possibility of communication with their environment. Most of them died. Furthermore, today sensory deprivation is probably still used as a form of torture and pressure on prisoners. Also, patients who are not able to move experience results of sensory deprivation. It is a method which was and is used in very different circumstances and which also sometimes just happens.

11 See also Solomon, P.; Kleeman, S. T. (1971): Sensory Deprivation. In: The American Journal of Psychiatry. 11/1971. Vol. 127, pp. 1546-1547.

12 Unknown (1971): Sensory Deprivation. In: The Lancet. 7736/1971. Vol. 298, p. 1244.

2.2 Where does one experience that?

There are many different circumstances under which people experience sensory deprivation. We restrict ourselves in this article to:

- silence in space
- self-experiment: isolation tanks
- punishment: Guantanamo
- illness: Locked-in-Syndrome

In the following chapters this article will try to connect those situations to each other in describing what sensory deprivation is able to do to a person and how it alters the texture of consciousness.

3. Silence in space and what it has to do with sensory deprivation

In space sensory deprivation occurs due to the reduction of stimuli of mainly two senses. The floating of the bodies in the weightlessness has been investigated in isolation tanks. (see next chapter) Here, we will only discuss the silence in space.

Due to the absence of any atmosphere, it is totally silent in space. The most quiet place on earth is the anechoic chamber in the Orfield Laboratory which is located in Minneapolis, Minnesota. The acoustic chamber is comprised of 3.3-foot-thick acoustic wedges made out of fiberglass, double walls of insulated steel and foot-thick concrete, which enables it to be 99.99 % sound absorbent. No one can stand more than 45 minutes inside Orfield Laboratory's ultra-silent anechoic chamber. The NASA has sent astronauts inside in order to figure out ways to help them to adapt better to outer space, which can be thought of as a massive anechoic chamber. To ratchet up the sensory deprivation experience, they are even put into a water-filled tank kept inside the room to determine how long it takes before hallucinations take place and whether they could work through it.

Aspects of sensory deprivation in space are described as well in the motion picture "Gravity". In this film the main character Dr. Ryan Stone is an astronaut from the USA. She gets seperated from the space ship during a repair outside of the ship. In consequence of this accident she finds herself floating in space totally uncontrolled. With the 3D-effect of the movie and the allround-perspective of the camera, the motion picture illustrates the circumstances of space with its absence of gravity and the total silence. The astronaut seems desperate as she keeps floating in

13 Check their homepage for pictures and further information: http://www.orfieldlabs.com/researchtour4.html (latest visit: 01/27/2014)

14 http://www.smartplanet.com/blog/thinking-tech/quietest-place-on-earth-causes-hallucinations/ (latest visit: 01/27/2014)

15 Cuaron, Alfonso (2013): Gravity. Warner Bros. Pictures. UK, USA.

the endless space, which is shown by her fast breathing. The absence of any sound causes helplessness and she tries to contact her colleagues on earth and in space without success. During this uncontrollable floating, her own breathing is all she can hear. Apart from that it is totally silent. Panic overcomes her and still it is clear that she is absolutely dependent on her helpless body. The movie tries to show the importance of sound and balance. "Gravity" illustrates also how quickly people in despair can get hallucinations when they cannot use their hearing sense. At one point she decides to die, then she hallucinates the presence of her colleague who gives her advice with which she could return to earth. Due to the astronaut's hallucination one can see that silence in space can evoke results of sensory deprivation. In this case it is used to motivate the figure to survive.

4. Self-experiments: Sensory deprivation in Isolation tanks

Some authors used drugs and other methods to expand their minds and get another view on consciousness itself. Aldous Huxley meticulously describes his self-experiment with psychedelic drugs in "The Doors of Perception". [16] He tries to reach a state where he can enter the "inner world described by Blake".[17] Neuroscientist John C. Lilly, the pioneer of sensory deprivation, used so called isolation tanks to deprive senses. In his autobiographical works he writes about this experience:

> *I found the isolation tank was a hole in the universe. I gradually began to see through to another reality. It scared me. I didn't know about alternate realities at that time, but I was experiencing them right and left without any LSD.* [18]

An isolation tank is a lightless, soundproof, temperature regulated tank, inside which salt is dissolved in water. Persons inside it are floating in water at skin temperature and have the illusion of being "weightless" like in space. The weightless feeling comes from the salt and the temperature regulated water. Due to this it is not possible anymore to orient oneself especially when face masks are worn. [19]

16 Huxley, A. (2011): The Doors of Perception. Thinking Ink: London, New York, Sydney.
17 ibid, p. 4.
18 Lilly, J. C. (1988): The scientist. A metaphysical autobiography. Ronin: Oakland. Between p. 121 and 123.
19 Lilly, J. C. (1956): Mental Effects of Reduction of Ordinary Levels of Physical Stimuli on Intact, Healthy Persons. In: Psychiatric Research Reports. 5/1956: http://www.planetpuna.com/Lilly%20Papers/40.%20LILLY,%20JOHN%20C.%201956.pdf (latest visit: 01/29/2014)

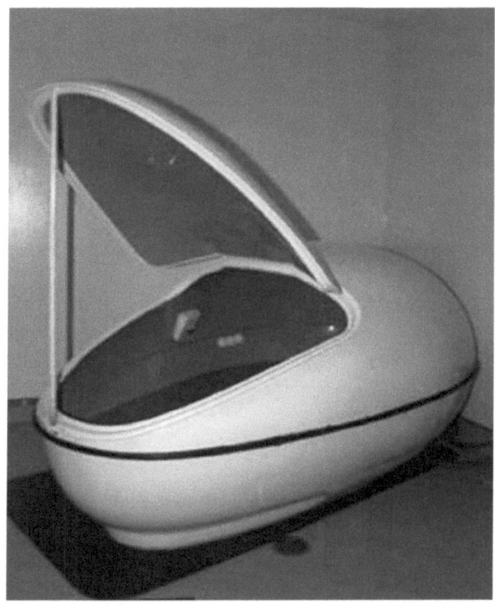

▲ Fig. 1: Isolation tank

Isolation tanks were originally called sensory deprivation tanks and were first used by John C. Lilly in 1954. At the US National Institute of Mental Health (NIMH),[21] Lilly commenced experiments with sensory deprivation. In neurophysiology there had been an open question as to what keeps the brain going and about the origin of its energy sources. One idea was that the energy sources are biological and internal and do not depend on the outside environment. It was argued that if all stimuli are cut off from the brain it would go to sleep. Lilly decided to test this hypothesis and, with this in mind, created an environment which totally isolated an individual from external stimulation: the sensory deprivation tank. With the tank he studied the origin of consciousness and its relation to the brain. [22]

The physicist and Nobel prize winner Richard Feynman described hallucinations and out-of-body experiences[23] while using a sensory deprivation tank. He describes it in his book "Surely You're Joking Mr. Feynman!"[24] Feynman was invited to try the isolation tank at John Lilly's home after Lilly attended one of Feynman's popular lectures on quantum mechanics.

20 Vartanian O. and P. Suedfeld (2011): The Effect of the Flotation Version of Restricted Environmental Stimulation Technique (REST) on Jazz Improvisation. In: Music and Medicine: http://mmd.sagepub.com/content/early/2011/05/05/1943862111407640 (latest visit: 01/30/2014)

21 See also US National Institute of Mental Health: http://www.nimh.nih.gov/index.shtml (latest visit: 01/27/2014)

22 Lilly: Mental Effects of Reduction of Ordinary Levels of Physical Stimuli on Intact, Healthy Persons.

23 Out-of-body experiences are reported by persons who are close to death or believe that they are close to death. They observe their own body as if they were another person. Many patients with a locked-in syndrome have also such experiences. See also Pantke: Locked-in. Gefangen im eigenen Körper, pp. 13-14.

24 Feynman et al. (1985): Surely You're Joking, Mr. Feynman! Adventures of a Curious Character. W W Norton: New York.

5. Punishment: Guantanamo and what the treatment of its prisoners has in common with sensory deprivation

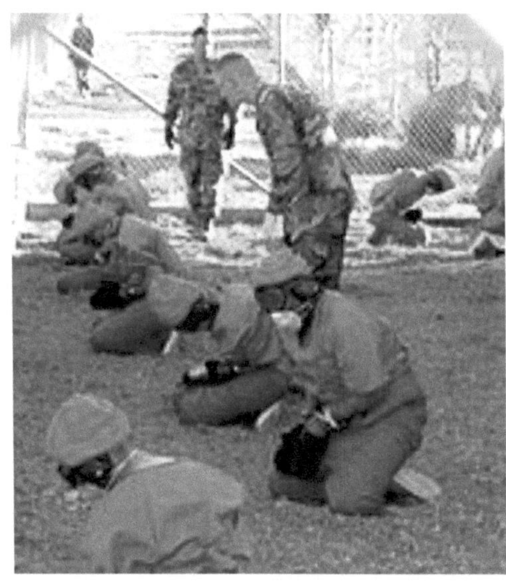

▲ Fig. 2: "Detainees in camp jumpsuits sit in a holding area under the watchful eyes of Military Police at Camp X-Ray at Naval Base Guantanamo Bay, Cuba, during in-processing to the temporary detention facility on Jan. 11, 2002. The detainees will be given a basic physical exam by a doctor, to include a chest x-ray and blood samples drawn to assess their health."[28]

The United States Naval Station Guantanamo Bay is located on 45 square miles (120 km^2) of land and water at Guantanamo Bay, Cuba. It was leased by the United States for the use as a naval station in the Cuban-American treaty of 1903. Since 1959 the Cuban government has consistently protested against the US presence at Guantanamo Bay and called the treaty illegal under modern international law. In January 2002 work was begun to extend the base into an internment camp for prisoners who were sent there by the US American state for being 'unlawful combatants' in their eyes.[25] In an Amnesty International report from 2005 Guantanamo was called "the gulag of our times".[26] US-president Barack Obama promised in his presidential elections in 2008 to fight for the closure of the camp[27], which has not yet happened.

In this chapter we cannot and will not discuss whether there is torture in Guantanamo. We only describe what can be seen on a photo published on the internet by an officer of the US army (see Fig. 2). In this photo prisoners are shown in camp clothes, with breathing masks, blindfolds, hearing protection, gloves and tied up hands and feet in a kneeling position.

25 See also http://en.wikipedia.org/wiki/Guantanamo_Bay_Naval_Base (latest vistit: 01/27/2014)

26 Kahn, I. (2005): Amnesty International Report 2005. Speech by Irene Khan at Foreign Press Association.

27 List of election promises and their status quo: http://www.politifact.com/truth-o-meter/promises/ (latest visit: 01/28/2014)

28 Photo by Petty Officer 1st Class Shane T. Mccoy/U.S. Department of Defense, via Reuters.

Torture is officially denied by the US-government[29], nevertheless, there is the suspicion that this treatment is rather a part of questionings which should break every psychic normality via sensory deprivation. Sensory deprivation is a subtle, but very effective method of torture and can be used as a brainwashing method. It is for example used in the form of isolation custody. With the method of isolation an attempt is made to achieve the greatest possible screening of all senses (eyes, ears, mouth, nose, hands, feet, skin). Sensory deprivation belongs to the methods of torture which cause no evident tracks on the body. The so called "white torture" is, according to some sources, the most used form of torture worldwide today. [30]

Anyone who has ever tried to close the eyes for more than a few minutes, knows that an awkward feeling sets in immediately. Imagining what this feeling must be like with many senses deprived and under enormous pressure and/or agony, depicts how important our senses are in order to feel connected to the world around us. [31]

6. Illness: Locked-in-Syndrome and what it has in common with sensory deprivation

The previous chapters have shown that the constraint or deprivation of senses has a huge influence on our conscious perception. For many people the experience of being in an isolation tank or in an anechoic chamber leads to hallucinations, for which many examples can be found in the article by Lilly.[32] One possibility to "use" sensory deprivation is the so called "white torture" which does not leave any signs of it on the body (see chapter 5). The appearance of hallucinations can be explained with the constrained flow of information to the brain with which it has to assimilate.

In all of the named examples above, a cutback of one or more senses takes place, which limits the flow of information to the brain. Except for this external limitation of information flow to the brain, it can also be limited by the body itself. This happens e.g. when someone suffers from the Locked-in-Syndrome.

29 See also http://news.bbc.co.uk/2/hi/americas/4782594.stm (latest visit: 01/23/2014)

30 See also http://listverse.com/2013/10/19/10-gruesome-torture-devices-used-in-modern-times/ (latest visit: 01/25/2014)

31 BBC report with volunteers who undergo sensory deprivation: http://www.bbc.co.uk/sn/tvradio/programmes/horizon/broadband/tx/isolation/ (latest visit: 01/27/2014)

32 Lilly: Mental Effects of Reduction of Ordinary Levels of Physical Stimuli on Intact, Healthy Persons.

6.1 The syndrome

The Locked-in-Syndrome is a serious neurological disease, which shows effects similar to sensory deprivation in the beginning stage.

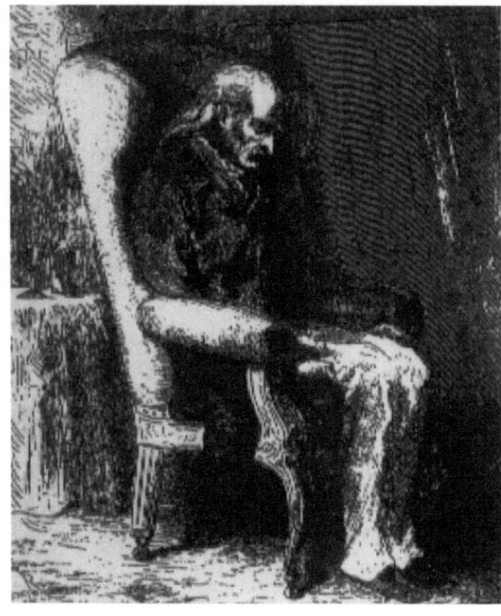

▲ Fig. 3: Mr. Noitier de Villefort in the "The Count of Monte Cristo"

It was first described vividly in 1844, by Alexandre Dumas in "The Count of Monte Cristo."[35] Herein Dumas depicted Mr. Noitier de Villefort as "a corpse with living eyes." [37] Mr. Noitier had been in this state for several years, and he could only communicate by blinking with his eyes. His granddaughter pointed at words in a dictionary and he indicated with his eyes the words he wanted. There is also another character in the book, who might have had a Locked-in-Syndrome.[38]

It took more than 100 years for the medical world to investigate this disease systematically. In 1966 Plum and Posner described the Locked-in-Syndrome for patients who are awake and conscious but paralyzed[39], except for vertical movements of the eye. This action can be used for communication. A mortality rate of 60% is reported.[40] The rehabilitation outcome is unclear, but there is data which gives hope, that the earlier the rehabilitation begins, the better the outcome will be for the patient.[41] Patients are treated like those with a stroke.

33 For further information, please check the homepages of the french organisation ALIS (association locked-in syndome, www.club-internet.fr/alis) and the german organisation LIS e.V. (Locked-in Syndom e.V. www.locked-in-syndrom.org).

34 Laureys, S. et al.: The Locked-in-Syndrome.

35 Dumas, A. [first published between 1844 and 46 in: Journal des Débates] (2012): The Count of Monte Cristo. Penguin Classics: London.

37 See also chapter "Noitier de Villefort" in Dumas, A.: The Count of Monte Cristo.

38 Williams, AN. (2003): Cerebrovascular disease in Dumas' "The Count of Monte Cristo". In: J R Soc Med 96/2003, pp. 412 -414.

39 Plum, F. and J. B. Posner (4. ed./2007): The Diagnosis of Stupor and Coma. Oxford University Press: New York.

40 Laureys, S. et al.: The Locked-in-Syndrome.

41 See also Smith, E. and Delargy, M. (2005): Locked-in-Syndrome. British Medical Journal. 2/2005. Vol. 330, pp. 406–409.

Many remain 100% dependent on assistance. Some patients with Locked-in-Syndrome can walk and speak again, overcome some of their physical restrictions and live independently. [42]

6.2 Patients voices

In 1995, Jean-Dominique Bauby, aged 43 and editor in chief of the fashion magazine Elle, had a stroke followed by a Locked-in-Syndrome. Bauby wanted to show the world that the Locked-in-Syndrome does not prevent patients from writing a book. He dictated it, letter by letter, to a lector from the publishing company who recited a frequency-ordered alphabet until Bauby chose a letter by blinking his left eyelid once to signify "yes"(see also chapter "the alphabet" in "The diving bell and the butterfly"). His book became a bestseller around the world and served as a template for a motion picture under the name "Assigné à résidence" by Jean-Jacques Beineix[43] in 1997 and some years later by Julian Schnabel.[44]

However there is more than this text constructing an inner life of patients suffering from Locked-in-Syndrome. The patient Karl-Heinz Pantke has written his own account. All these texts have in common: the deprivation of the sense of motion and the inability to communicate this to the environment, which let patients experience a "dream world".

Mr. Knoop writes:

> *Somehow I was pressed into a knight's armour made out of stone. My liberty of action didn't seem to exist. I trudged myself into water, where I immediately sank onto the ground. To my own astonishment, I wasn't the only one who tried to move in a knight's armour under water. A whole army of petrified soldiers was there. I tried to get their solidarity which worked immediately. We formed an insurmountable wall. A whole army of petrified knights.*[45]

42 See also Ostrum, A. E. (1994): The "locked-in" syndrome – comments from a survivor. In: Brain Injury. 1/1994. Vol. 8. Informa Healthcare.

43 See also Beineix, J.-J. (1997): Assigné à résidence. France.

44 Schnabel, Julian (2007): The Diving Bell and the Butterfly. Pathé, Miramax. France, USA.

45 Knoop, F. In: Wahrnehmungsverschiebungen – Patienten berichten [change in Perception - reports of patients] In: Metamorphose. Beobachtungen zum Zusammenhang von Bewegung und Wahrnehmung bei motorischen Einschränkungen durch Krankheiten. [Observations of the connection between movement and perception by motor restrictions]. Eine Publikation von LIS e.V.: Berlin. Ed. Kühn, C.; Mrosack, G.; Scharbert, G; Pantke, K.-H. Vol. 2. 2002, p.11.

Mr. Müller writes:

> *I didn't understand my total paralysis and speechlessness. The edge of the antidekubitus-matress was quite high. I saw it as living or electrical dummies which lay in my bed. I will now describe how that felt. The dummies got hold of my arms and legs. My lower legs were entangled by the dummies `legs so that I could not turn around. The head was also hand-held by them, nothing was possible anymore.*[46]

Both patients said that they were sleeping. After massive brain damage which led to a Locked-in-Syndrome, there are no clear borders between hallucination, dream and reality anymore. Karl-Heinz Pantke himself illustrates that:

> *As I lay on the Intensive Care Unit, I saw a man lie completely still, and slowly die. I also saw his dead body being brought away. That was real. But the subsequent funeral was a hallucination. In the moment of experiencing something, reality and hallucination cannot be distinguished. But because of the fact that I could not leave my bed due to the Locked-in-Syndrome, I can clearly say that every perception which took place outside of the bed, must have been a hallucination.*[47]

The voices of the non moving patients with the Locked-in-Syndrome illustrate clearly, how a brain reacts on being deprived of motion-information for a long time. Of course the human body does not have an organ responsible for motion. But the position of arms and legs relatively to the body gets determined continiously as we move.[48] Also, a performed motion generates a feedback to the brain without it being realised consciously. In the Locked-in-Syndrome, all this information ceases to exist from one moment to the other. In this sense, the term 'sensory deprivation' can be used in the Locked-in-Syndrome.

The processing in the brain and its consciousness depends on the input of the senses. A healthy person is not aware of this condition. But for a person recovering from a Locked-in-Syndrome, who can walk again, a change in consciousness can be observed. While a healthy person does not spare much attention on a daily action like walking, for a patient recovering from a Locked-in-Syndrome walking is similar to an artistic performance. The main challenge is to keep the

46 Müller, G. (2002): Im Reich der Halluzinationen. Gefangen im Ich nach dem Schlaganfall. Das Locked-in-Syndrom. [In the Empire of hallucinations. Imprisoned in your own body after a stroke. The Locked-in-Syndrome] LIS e. V.: Berlin, p. 12.

47 Pantke, K.-H. (2009): Locked-in. Gefangen im eigenen Körper. [Locked-in. Imprisoned in your own body]. Mabuse: Frankfurt a.M, pp. 25-26.

48 Leyh, A. (2011): Sich selbst fühlen. [Experiencing yourself] Website: www.dasGehirn.info – ein Projekt der Gemeinnützigen Hertie-Stiftung, der Neurowissenschaftlichen Gesellschaft e. V. in Zusammenarbeit mit dem ZKM (Zentrum für Kunst und Medientechnologie Karlsruhe). http://dasgehirn.info/wahrnehmen/fuehlen-koerper/sich-selbst-fuehlen/view/ (latest visit: 01/27/2014)

body in balance. To achieve this, the sight must be reliable. If the light is suddenly switched off, for example on a staircase, the person risks falling while walking. Due to the missing information from the visual sense, the balance gets out of control. [personal information from a member of LIS e.V.] This example shows how close the brain and the input from the senses are related to each other.

7. Conclusion

We have shown that sensory deprivation can occur under many different circumstances. But no matter whether a person has the Locked-in-Syndrome, floats in an isolation tank or experiences silence in space, most of them seem to show similar reactions. They have periods of panic, anxiety, they get sleepy and have hallucinations. In this sense, the texture of the environment influences the texture of human consciousness. The less there is in the outer world, the more the inner world of a person seems to wake.

Surely there is a huge difference in the circumstances of the individual in the deprived situation. It is not the same being a prisoner or a volunteer. Sensory deprivation pared with sleeplessness and agony probably leads to psychotic episodes and hallucinations more quickly than in a situation when someone opts to be in an isolation tank just for fun and for as long as he or she wants.

But still, the human brain seems to need permanent and non-monotone information from the environment in order to stabilize the psyche. Maybe for locked-in-patients hallucinations also seem to be a helpful tool to survive the horrible state of total paralysis. Maybe it can be understood as a mechanism of survival in unbearable situations.

We cannot define what consciousness is, but we have shown that a definition without our environment is impossible. Nontheless people – like the patients in chapter 6.2 – try to communicate their hallucinations, dreams, illusions, imaginations, phantasies, realities out of the body into the world via text. This can be read as a texture of consciousness – an expression of a locked-in spirit. It is also a form of therapy to depict the conditions inside the body. The dream of being able to use every sense helps to focus the aim and distracts the person from their fateful position. As Jean-Dominique Bauby puts it:

> *There is so much to do. You can wander off in space or in time, set out for Tierra del Fuego or for King Midas's court. You can visit the woman you love, slide down beside her and stroke her still-sleeping face. You can build castles in Spain, steal the Golden Fleece, discover Atlantis, realize your childhood dreams an adult ambitions.*[51]

49 See also Lilly, J. C. (1956): Mental Effects of Reduction of Ordinary Levels of Physical Stimuli on Intact, Healthy Persons.

50 See also Solomon, P.: Sensory Deprivation.

51 Bauby: The diving bell and the butterfly, p. 5.

8. Literature

8.1 References

Books and articles:

- Bauby, J. (1998): The diving bell and the butterfly. Vintage Books: New York.
- Dumas, A. (2012): The Count of Monte Cristo. Penguin Classics: London.
- Feynman et al. (1985): Surely You're Joking, Mr. Feynman! Adventures of a Curious Character. W W Norton: New York.
- Huxley, A. (2011): The Doors of Perception. Thinking Ink: London, New York, Sydney.
- Kahn, I. (2005): Amnesty International Report 2005. Speech by Irene Khan at Foreign Press Association. See also: http://www.amnesty.org/en/library/asset/POL10/014/2005/en/31217bcc-d4e5-11dd-8a23-d58a49c0d652/pol100142005en.html.
- Kühn, C.; Mrosack, G.; Scharbert, G; Pantke, K.-H. [Ed.]: Wahrnehmungsverschiebungen – Patienten berichten [change in Perception - reports of patients] In: Metamorphose. Beobachtungen zum Zusammenhang von Bewegung und Wahrnehmung bei motorischen Einschränkungen durch Krankheiten. [Observations of the connection between movement and perception by motor restrictions]. Eine Publikation von LIS e.V.: Berlin.Vol. 2. 2002.
- Laureys, S.; Pellas, F.; Eeckhout Van, P.; Ghorbel, S.; Schnakers, C.; Perrin, F.; Berré, J.; Faymonville, M.-E.; Pantke, K.-H.; Damas, F.; Lamy, M.; Moonen, G. and S. Goldman (2005): The Locked-in-Syndrome: What is it like to be conscious but paralyzed and voiceless? Prog Brain Res. 2005. Issue 150, pp. 495-511. See also: http://www.coma.ulg.ac.be/papers/LIS/2005_PBR_vol150_495_511.pdf.
- Lilly, J. C. (1956): Mental Effects of Reduction of Ordinary Levels of Physical Stimuli on Intact, Healthy Persons. In: Psychiatric Research Reports. 5. See also: http://www.planetpuna.com/Lilly%20Papers/40.%20LILLY,%20JOHN%20C.%201956.pdf.
- Lilly, J. C. (1988): The scientist. A metaphysical autobiography. Ronin: Oakland.
- Locke, J. (2001): An essay concerning human understanding. Batoche: Kitchener.
- Metzinger, T (1995): Bewusstsein. Beiträge aus der Gegenwartsphilosophie. [Consciousness. Contributions from temporary philosophy.] Ed. Metzinger. Mentis: Paderborn.
- Müller, G. (2002): Im Reich der Halluzinationen. Gefangen im Ich nach dem Schlaganfall. Das Locked-in-Syndrom. [In the Empire of hallucinations. Imprisoned in your own body after a stroke. The Locked-in-Syndrome] LIS e. V.: Berlin.
- Ostrum, A. E. (1994): The "locked-in" syndrome – comments from a survivor. In: Brain Injury. 1/1994. Vol. 8. Informa Healthcare.
- Pantke, K.-H. (2009): Locked-in. Gefangen im eigenen Körper. [Locked-in. Imprisoned in your own body]. Mabuse: Frankfurt a.M.
- Pistorius, M. (2011): Ghost boy. Simon&Schuster: London.
- Plum, F. and J. B. Posner (4. ed./2007): The Diagnosis of Stupor and Coma. Oxford University Press: New York.
- Prinz, J.J. (2012): Could Consciousness be Physical? The Brain Maintained. Oxford University Press: Oxford.
- Sacks, O. (2013): Hallucinations. Vintage Books: New York. 2013.
- Smith, E. and Delargy, M. (2005): Locked-in-Syndrome. British Medical Journal. 2/2005. Vol. 330, pp. 406–409. See also: http://www.ncbi.nlm.nih.gov/pmc/articles/PMC549115/.
- Solomon, P.; Kleeman, S. T. (1971): Sensory Deprivation. In: The American Journal of Psychiatry. 11/1971. Vol. 127, pp. 1546-1547.
- Tononi, G. (2004) An information integration theory of consciousness. In: BMC Neuroscience 5/ 2004. Issue 42. See also: http://www.architalbiol.org/aib/article/viewFile/15056/23165867.
- Unknown (1971): Sensory Deprivation. In: The Lancet. 7736/1971. Vol. 298.
- Welsh, C. (2007): Die „Dunkelheit hinter dem Stirnportal". Begegnungen von Literatur und Hirnforschung zwischen 1800 und 2000. [The „Darkness behind our fronthead". Encounters between literature and brain research between 1800-2000.] In: Jahrbuch für Literatur und Medizin, vol. 1, p. 95-111.
- Williams, AN. (2003): Cerebrovascular disease in Dumas' "The Count of Monte Cristo". In: J R Soc Med 96/2003, pp. 412 -414. See also: http://www.ncbi.nlm.nih.gov/pmc/articles/PMC539579/.

Linklist:

- ALIS' Website: Association locked-in syndome: www.club-internet.fr/alis
- Article about Guantanamo Prison: http://en.wikipedia.org/wiki/Guantanamo_Bay_Naval_Base
- Article on "White Torture": http://listverse.com/2013/10/19/10-gruesome-torture-devices-used-in-modern-times/
- Information about the anechoic chamber: http://www.smartplanet.com/blog/thinking-tech/quietest-place-on-earth-causes-hallucinations/
- Information about Isolation: http://www.bbc.co.uk/sn/tvradio/programmes/horizon/broadband/tx/isolation/
- LIS e.V.'s Website: Locked-in Syndom e.V.: www.locked-in-syndrom.org
- List of election promises and their status quo: http://www.politifact.com/truth-o-meter/promises/
- Orfield Laboratories' Website: http://www.orfieldlabs.com/researchtour4.html
- Unknown: Top US official denies 'torture' Article about the Deny of torture in Guantanamo. BBC News. 2006: http://news.bbc.co.uk/2/hi/americas/4782594.stm
- US National Institute of Mental Health's Website: http://www.nimh.nih.gov/index.shtml

Motion Pictures and Information Videos:

- Trumbo, Dalton (1971): Johnny got his gun.
- Beineix, J.-J. (1997): Assigné à résidence. France.
- Cuaron, Alfonso (2013): Gravity. Warner Bros. Pictures. UK, USA.
- Leyh, A. (2011): Sich selbst fühlen. [Experiencing yourself] Website: www.dasGehirn.info – ein Projekt der Gemeinnützigen Hertie-Stiftung, der Neurowissenschaftlichen Gesellschaft e. V. in Zusammenarbeit mit dem ZKM (Zentrum für Kunst und Medientechnologie Karlsruhe). http://dasgehirn.info/wahrnehmen/fuehlen-koerper/sich-selbst-fuehlen/view/.
- Schnabel, Julian (2007): The Diving Bell and the Butterfly. Pathé, Miramax. France, USA.

Photos:

- Detainees in Guantanamo photographed by Petty Officer 1st Class Shane T. Mccoy/ U.S. Department of Defense, via Reuters.
- Vartanian O. and P. Suedfeld (2011): The Effect of the Flotation Version of Restricted Environmental Stimulation Technique (REST) on Jazz Improvisation. In: Music and Medicine: http://mmd.sagepub.com/content/early/2011/05/05/1943862111407640.

Merleau-Ponty and the Texture of Consciousness

by

Mark Fielding

Of all the classic problems of Philosophy it is arguably the case that the most intractable is that of consciousness. Typically, this is presented in terms of offering a satisfactory account of the 'felt' quality of experience. In addition to the experience of the world through the senses, and other mental states, such as emotions, there is a quality to these states which, it is claimed, defies characterisation without factoring in an ownership – these are not simply pains, for example, they are my pains. This view – and the range of solutions proposed to account for it – makes it seem like the problem is to explain the fact of how we do connect to the world in this very unusual, if not unique, way.

Philosophy has tended to view its role as providing an account of how radically distinct entities – mind and body – interact. This is most clearly presented in Descartes' claims about each as a kind of 'stuff'. So, explaining how a mental thing, for example, a 'thought' and a physical thing, for example, a table, can interact is the problem of explaining how two distinct substances can interact. Typically, this presents the difficulty of finding the conceptual tools which are neutral between the two kinds of thing. One possible candidate is the notion of causation. It fits quite easily into our everyday way of talking about mind -world interaction. The difficulty is that the concept is usually understood as explaining the interaction between physical objects – if you hit a nail with a hammer this causes the nail to be driven into the wood, say. Mental things are, for Descartes, quite distinct from physical things and so using the concept of causation to explain the interaction depends on identifying the ways in which the mind can causally impinge on the world (and vice versa). This will have to be done via some view about how the mind is causally linked to the brain and Descartes' suggestion was that the pineal gland provided this point of contact. Of course, that is itself a physical thing and so doesn't obviously solve the problem. Although other approaches have been offered since, each has its own problems, which perhaps suggests a different way of thinking about the mind is required.

Merleau-Ponty was one of the most important exponents of the branch of Philosophy known as Phenomenology. Beginning with Edmund Husserl and his student, Martin Heidegger, the task of philosophical thought is to provide a proper description of the interaction between our world and our sense of it. The central contention is that, in contrast to Descartes and those following in his footsteps, this apparent separation of mind and body is a secondary phenomenon. Our primary way of engaging with the world is as participants in it. We do not primarily experience the world as something other than us – we experience ourselves as part of the world. Adopting a phrase from Heidegger, Merleau-Ponty describes this state as Being-in-the-World.

Whereas, from the modern point of view of experience, we are passive recipients of the world though our senses, the phenomenologist suggests that perception is an activity. Furthermore, this is not the activity of a radically and problematically separate entity – a Mind – but is instead the relation to a world in which we are already involved – as body.

This view doesn't deny that we can see ourselves as separate and special in relation to the world and other, simpler, organisms which live in it, but suggests that we cut ourselves off from thinking about the more basic relation mentioned above. It isn't possible to provide a solution to the problem of explaining the link between Mind and World because the more basic description of ourselves, as embodied with our way of being as Being-in-the-World. Finding inspiration in his reading of Husserl, Merleau-Ponty suggests that consciousness isn't a matter of "I think" but "I can".

This isn't to deny that our consciousness interacts with the world, as, strictly speaking, it is entirely interwoven with it, through the possibilities for thought and action which we possess as embodied. The characteristics of our bodies creates an "atmosphere" in which we engage with our existence as subjects. Merleau-Ponty was convinced that this necessitates ways of regarding ourselves which is irreducibly social, rather than simply biological.

What kinds of constraints and possibilities does this view present us with? Well, following Freud, Merleau-Ponty suggests that there is an irreducible sexual element to our existence. However, against Freud's reductionist description of ourselves as purely biological creatures with 'drives' and 'instincts' with which we are more or less capable of engaging, Merleau-Ponty claims that to make sense of the kinds of problems Freud identifies it is necessary to see ourselves as actively engaged with our environment, attempting to deal with problems which our existence presents us with as embodied beings. Our bodies are both the basis of our engagement with others and the basis of our ability to make sense that engagement. As we develop we find new and possibly more successful ways of integrating the requirements of our bodily existence. We form and re-form our selves in carrying out this task. Of course, as the circumstances of our embodiment change and are changed by this interaction, we are never in a position of having, as it were, caught up with ourselves – and we are never in a position where we have exhausted our past in this activity of creating ourselves anew. Insofar as we continue to interact with others, in pursuit of our various projects, we are works-in-progress. Rather than Descartes' magnificently isolated and passive "I" Merleau-Ponty offers us a vision of our consciousness as thoroughly 'outwardly-directed' and actively engaged 'being-with-others'. We are incapable of defining ourselves once-and-for-all because we are nothing other than this on-going engagement.

One of the more interesting implications of the above view is that we are not straightforwardly in a position of knowledge about ourselves. When we reflect on how we feel about someone, or about how a situation has developed, this is not simply an exercise in extracting a 'fact' from our internal record. Rather, it can be better thought about as a kind of adventure of discovery – and as with all adventures, there can be surprising and challenging aspects to the activity. We discover something in conducting this investigation, and what that is can have far-reaching consequences for both our sense of ourselves and our view of possible ways of behaving. It's the difference between contemplating a (mental) object stored somewhere in our mind and reflecting upon our lived experience.

A critical component in this picture of ourselves which is developing is that, rather than being the kind of thing which exists in a way which is separate from the world, we are a part of it, and so are located in a place and, crucially, at a time. Temporality is the background to all of our engagements with the world, as we encounter it as part of projects in which we are engaged, as the result of a view about what has been, and projecting ourselves into a future which is to come. The need to find a meaning in the past which will be involved in how we orientate ourselves to our future indicates that without time, we cannot have existence: our being-in-the-world is temporal. As we having our being as embodied, our past isn't simply a matter of contemplation for us, it is realised in our bodies which are, as he says in The Phenomenology of Perception, "the eloquent relic of an existence".

One of the most unfortunate aspects of the sense of ourselves offered by Descartes is that our knowledge of others is suddenly problematic. If the foundation of all knowledge is the "I" of the cogito, which is capable of occupying this task only because it is incapable of being doubted, then our relation to others is easily doubted. Descartes suggests that it's perfectly possible that the others we encounter who appear to be other minds, might perfectly well be complex automata which we (wrongly) imagine to be bearers of a cogito as we are. There is only one consciousness about which I can be certain, and that's me!

Contra this view, Merleau-Ponty's claim about the embodied nature of our being proposes that each of us has the same basis on which to be regarded as a subject. We are subjects with others first of all. My world is a shared world, rather than a private viewing gallery with space only for one. The sense I make of this world, the meanings I reach for in understanding myself, are established first of all in the social setting. We live in a world we make with others and we form and re-form ourselves in the atmosphere provided by that social setting. He sometimes describes this setting as the "interworld" and its most important constituting element is language. We exist, as subjects, in a world which is made sense of primarily in terms of language.
Our ability to make sense of ourselves is, at the same time, dependent on our ability to make sense of others. The problem of understanding ourselves is not a distinct and more intractable problem than understanding others – it's enabled as a possibility by the shared setting of all acts of understanding. Of course, as mentioned above, this is best viewed as an open-ended and on-going process, but now we must adjust the view of how time is an element in this process. It isn't now a matter of my past and my future, but of our past and our future. We are, as things which have our being-in-the-world, collectively located.

As a result of this, all of the points which have been made about us, as individual subjects, are also true of us as a whole. To speak of freedom, for example, is, by implication, to speak of freedom for us all. This stitches together his phenomenological treatment of the individual with his political and social thought.

To conclude, it's useful to consider how this way of understanding ourselves in explicitly related to the Arts in Merleau-Ponty's work. Very broadly, the Arts, like Philosophy, is vital in its capacity to engage with the world before we complicate and confuse ourselves with various general descriptions of things – Descartes being a classic example. If done well, all forms of artistic expression can achieve this clarification as they present the world to us before we think about it. Its advantage is not that we can be more accurate in how we relate to the world, but that we can acquire new ways of seeing it. They do this not through formulating new concepts, but by allowing a difference in the way in which events are depicted. In making it possible for the world to appear differently to us, Art and Philosophy add new textures to our consciousness.

Thoughts without a Thinker

by

Robert Silman

Consciousness is something which characterises being sentient of three textures. i) Feelings (e.g. pain, pleasure, hunger, sexual desire, friendship, beauty, loyalty, etc.) which may or may not be accompanied by thoughts or acts. ii) Thoughts (e.g. dreams, ambitions, plans, fantasies, images, abstractions, etc.) which may or may not be related to feelings or acts. iii) Ourselves, as sentient beings.

The first two are not reserved to humans. When a dog wags its tail he is communicating a feeling resembling happiness. We cannot know if a dog has thoughts as distinct from feelings because he can't tell us, though he probably does. We know humans have thoughts because we have the evidence of our own thoughts which are independent of any accompanying act; and because other humans constantly communicate their thoughts to us outside of any accompanying act apart from the act of communication itself. Indeed the very fact of me writing this essay is an example of a thought (or thoughts) on my part and the only act associated with it is the one whereby I translate the thoughts into script; and if someone reads this, the reader will have evidence that the writer had recorded some thoughts (however imperfect).

Finally we know that humans are conscious of more than thoughts. Humans are conscious of themselves as thinking beings. I am conscious of myself as "me"; and others tell me that "I" am "you" for "them" and "they" are their own "me". Indeed if someone loses a sense of their own identity, or is incapable of recognising the identity of others, it is considered a sign of major mental illness. Self-consciousness is the moment when I see (and judge) myself; when I can think the thought and say the words "I" and "me". Consciousness, in its highest form, is synonymous with self-consciousness.

1) Thoughts

What are thoughts? In particular what are abstract thoughts, i.e. thoughts which are not necessarily associated with a feeling or an act? "Thinking" and "thought" are not synonymous. Though I (and Descartes!) know more or less what I mean when I say "I think", can my thoughts (i.e. the subjects/objects of my thinking) exist outside my brain and the brain of others? In other words can thoughts exist outside of someone/something thinking them? We seem to belittle thoughts which are programmed; i.e. when we can see how the thought arose. So when a computer informs us of something we didn't know, we don't say that the computer had a "thought" and we certainly don't say it had a conscious thought. But though I am conscious of my own thoughts and those of others, thoughts are not the same as my consciousness of them. It is possible to conceive of thoughts existing without anyone or anything being conscious of them, just as it is possible to conceive of trees and flowers continuing to exist in a universe without anyone ever seeing them. Let's take the example of this essay. I am thinking about this paragraph and my thoughts are being translated into words on my computer. But when I close my computer and cease to think these thoughts, do the thoughts cease to exist? Obviously they can be recalled when I reopen my computer, at which time I may (or may not) modify them. But if I cease to exist, if my thoughts cease to exist inside my brain, the thoughts expressed in this paragraph still survive so long as my computer survives and so long as this paragraph is able to be retrieved from my computer. And this must be true whether or not some thinker, other than me, opens my computer to read these thoughts. It must be true that these thoughts can survive without a thinker; otherwise these thoughts would cease to exist between the acts of someone thinking them. But just as we know the vanishing lady is a magic trick; we have to solve the puzzle of where thoughts hide when they are not being thought!

So back to the question: "what is abstract thought?" It clearly does not mean thoughts which cannot have a concrete reality. Abstract thought (as we shall discuss later) is at its best when embedded in real matter. No, the definition of abstract thought, at least as far as this essay is concerned, is any thought which can exist outside a consciousness of it. Let's take an example of its opposite, a non-abstract thought. If I am hungry and I plan to satisfy my hunger and this engenders all sorts of thoughts as to how I can satisfy my hunger, these are thoughts that cease to have relevance outside of my consciousness of them or others consciousness of me. In other words they are thoughts which cannot bear any meaning without, in some form or other, referring to the sentient being who thought them. By contrast, the radical definition of an abstract thought which I am proposing is a thought which can exist outside of any sentient being actually thinking it.

Now you may think I'm being perverse with this definition. I have been arguing that this essay is "abstract thought" and yet, clearly, these thoughts are my thoughts. So how can I claim that abstract thoughts can exist without someone thinking them? Or, better still, how can I demonstrate the reality of thoughts without a thinker?

2) Interlocking Themes

This is where we move to several interlocking themes.

2.1 Entropy

In Physics, the first law of thermodynamics states that matter cannot be created or destroyed, and the second law states that every physical reaction in the universe contributes to entropy. This second law basically states that the energy of the universe is always being lost, it can never be increased. Energy conservation is just a way of slowing the dissipation of energy, it can never reverse it. If we create wind farms to capture the energy of the wind as electricity, we are conserving some small part of the energy of the wind; but the rest, the wind energy we fail to capture, simply dissipates. And the electricity we create will eventually itself be dissipated. Energy is a gradient, the ordering of matter; entropy is the opposite, it is the absence of a gradient, a sort of equilibrium where matter is in such disorder that nothing can be done. The second law is the affirmation that disorder always increases, heat always flows from hot to cold, energy is always being dissipated so that eventually everything will equilibrate and there will be no energy difference between different states of matter; and the universe will have entered a state of entropic doom.

2.2 Communication Theory

It might be worthwhile to digress into a related domain, Communication Theory. Shannon and Weaver's seminal theory of communication states that the meaning of a message can never be improved and can only be degraded when it is passed from point A to point B. In other words the task of the communication engineer is to reduce as far as is possible the interference with the message. Interference with a message is "noise". It could just as well be called entropy because it is essentially the same concept as the second law; i.e. order tending to disorder (and never the reverse) is essentially the same as a message being degraded by noise (and never the reverse).

2.3 Life

"What is Life?" asked Schroedinger. The answer is as short as the question. Life is a break on entropy. Living organisms are defined as living because they organise matter around them; i.e. they slow the process of entropy. Of course there is still a contribution towards entropy but it is less than without life. For every living plant that captures the sun's rays to mobilise its energy as chlorophyll, the second law is still intact because there must always be a greater loss of energy from the sun than can be captured and conserved by all the plants in the solar system. In other words life is like a biological wind farm; it cannot reverse entropy, but it does slow it down.

2.4 Knowledge

Now we arrive at Knowledge. I have talked about the first and second laws of thermodynamics. I have talked about Communication Theory and the nature of Life as a break on entropy. All this is scientific Knowledge, which is another way of saying that all this is a form of thought. Of course we only have these thoughts when we are thinking them but they are a different sort of thought from us thinking about when we're hungry and how we plan to deal with our hunger. These are, in a sense, universal thoughts, i.e. we don't think of these thoughts as being dependent on any particular thinker, we think of them as being dependent on their truth/validity or not. Also, though they are universal, that does not mean they are thoughts which can be thought by everyone. On the contrary, some of these thoughts are difficult to comprehend, and thinkers have to be trained and educated before they are capable of thinking them. Nor are they thoughts which are true/valid forever; on the contrary, they are thoughts which develop and improve with time, which can be passed and refined from generation to generation, and which, to use an unfashionable word, progress.

The astonishing thing about these thoughts which constitute the body of Knowledge which is science is that the one thought which has always remained out of bounds for the scientist is scientific thought itself. And here is where we come to the nub of my argument. I would argue that it has to be a basic premise of science that our scientific understanding of the universe must have arisen from the universe it is studying! Our Knowledge of the universe teaches us that the universe is created from energy and matter. Therefore we should acknowledge that this Knowledge must arise from the object of its Knowledge; i.e. Knowledge itself must have come from the energy and matter it is studying. In other words the one remaining immense gap in our Knowledge of matter is how Knowledge can be created from matter. So, just as the highest form of consciousness is self-consciousness, the highest form of science is self-science; i.e. a science which knows and understands how it has come into being, a science which can explain itself, the Knowledge of Knowledge.

But what is this Knowledge of Knowledge? I can dimly perceive where the answer might reside. It surely has to be rooted in the laws of Physics, there has to be an "equation" which relates energy to Knowledge. To explain what I mean, let us start with a practical example which, for me at least, is easier to develop. Let us take the example of the explorers, the Magellans, Cooks etc., who discovered the geography of the world. The energy required to map the world by those early explorers was much greater than the energy required to visit it by those who followed. Why? Because the followers were not travelling into the unknown, the original explorers had created a body of Knowledge which could save those that followed an unnecessary expense of energy. In other words, if I were to sail to Australia, I would not be re-discovering Australia. Discovery is a once and for all event. Once Knowledge is obtained, we can learn from it but we do not re-discover it. In terms of energy, the more we know (or can learn) in advance, the less we have to expend in the energy of discovery. As far as I know there are no "equations" which express this conservation of energy by Knowledge. But the fact that such conservation exists must mean there is some such formula. And any such formula would contribute to what I mean by "self-science".

Of course the problem of a self-science is much more complex than mapping the world. The discovery of land mass is as nothing compared to the discovery of the laws of physics! Newton and Einstein did not discover continents, they discovered abstractions about matter: and, once discovered, they are there to be "learnt" not "re-discovered" by others. And, of course, these abstract thoughts about the nature of matter have indeed been learnt and are currently being used to change the world; to slow down entropy by the use of technology based on these laws, and/or to increase entropy by weapons of mass destruction created on the back of these laws.

2.5 Maxwell's Demon

I say there must be an "equation" which links energy to Knowledge in much the same way as energy is linked to light and mass. I am no physicist and therefore am incapable providing the "Knowledge" equivalent of $E=mc^2$. However I do not want to use this as a lame excuse for not taking the argument further forward. I am capable of discerning some of the features of this equation. The one that stands out is Maxwell's Demon. In the 19th century Maxwell suggested a "demon" which might reverse the second law of thermodynamics. He argued that if you had two chambers filled with gas in equilibrium with each other and a trap door between the two, you could imagine that a demon might observe the atoms of gas hitting the trap door and open the trap to let hot into one side cold in the other and thereby reverse the second law. There have been two major objections to the demon: i) it does not exist; and ii) even if it did, the energy that the demon would have to expend in observing the atoms would be greater than the energy being conserved in opening or closing the trap and therefore the second law would still be intact. Now I am suggesting both these objections are wrong. Firstly, the demon does exist. The demon is scientific thought! Second, because the demon is science, the premise is incomplete. Though we can agree that there is more energy expended in an observation than can be gained from that observation, this is only true of the observation. It is not true of the Knowledge gained from the observation. In other words if the observation(s) gives rise to a set of rules, e.g. a law of physics, there is no need to repeat the observation(s). Knowledge replaces the need to repeat the observation(s). Once there is discovery, there is no need for re-discovery. And, just like with the explorers of old, the energy gained by the use of Knowledge can exceed the energy expended in obtaining that Knowledge. And, once we concede that Knowledge is a form of energy, the second law no longer holds true.

2.6 Mutation

You may think I am shirking the Big Question, the one which says if Knowledge comes from observation, how did matter/energy create the observer; i.e. the discoverers on the back of which Knowledge can accrete? The answer, of course, lies with the theory of evolution where unicellular primitive life has evolved into the human species capable of understanding the mechanisms of life. But the theory of evolution is itself a form of Maxwell's Demon. If we consider how life replicates itself, i.e. how it passes information from one generation to the next, it is via the genetic code. This is squarely in the realm of Communication Theory. The message (an intact genetic code) must be transmitted from organism to organism without interference from noise (disruption/destruction of the genetic code). For living organisms, the most dangerous form of noise is mutation where a piece of the genetic code is damaged or wrongly transcribed. If we apply Communication Theory to this transmission of information, Shannon and Weaver's law is valid because mutations are, in the vast majority of cases, harmful. They are indeed "noise" and can lead to the deterioration/death of the organism that receives the disrupted message. But (a big "but"!) some tiny number of mutations are not harmful. Indeed they are essential for a Darwinian evolution of the species to occur. Without mutation, i.e. without "noise", life could not have proceeded from the antediluvian unicellular organism to the human species.

Evolution depends on some tiny number of the random mutations produced by "noise" to be actually advantageous. From the millions of mutations, which occur over hundreds of millions of years and which create a disadvantage for the organisms which bear them, a tiny few result in an organism which is actually better equipped to cope with its environment than its parent or its peers. As a result this organism is preferentially selected and propagated. In other words, in a tiny number the disruption of the message by "noise" did not lead to a degradation of the message but to another message, a better message. We could argue that the totality of mutations which are harmful exceed those that are beneficial and therefore in the totality of the system noise/entropy gains. But this does not take into account the step change advantage that "noise" creates in leading us to the human species, the only living form capable of converting observation into Knowledge. And, just like with Maxwell's Demon, the energy garnered by humans via the accumulation of Knowledge may exceed the energy required to create the human species. And, just like the second law, Shannon and Weaver's law ceases to be valid because evolution depends on the conversion of "noise" to meaning; i.e. entropy to energy.

3) In the end was the Word.

I am not exactly sure what I am trying to say in this essay; but I will try to make it clearer, if only to myself, by summarising as best I can. Religion aside, we can all agree that life arose from matter. In other words, at some propitious environmental moment on this planet (about 3 billion years ago), matter became life; i.e. matter organised itself into a unicellular organism (or some even more primitive life form) to place a break on entropy. Religion aside, we can all agree that once life was established it evolved over the next 2 billion years to produce the human species; i.e. at various points during this period, via the accident of propitious mutation where "noise" produced a "better" message, primitive life advanced step by step to produce homo sapiens. Religion aside, we can all agree that over the last 200,000 years the primitive caveman has evolved to become our modern day scientist and thinker. But what we cannot yet agree is how this last stage was achieved. We can acknowledge that the human species has been able to convert observation into Knowledge, not just Knowledge for itself like a Pavlov dog, but Knowledge for its species. What we do not understand is how this is possible. The great remaining mystery is: "What is Knowledge?"

I am arguing that Knowledge is not relative; i.e. not all forms of Knowledge are equal. A knowledge of the gods and their powers by the Oracle of the Ancient Greeks is not the same as Knowledge of the theory of relativity. The first is not dependent on truth/validity, the second is. The value of the first, in energy terms, is close to zero; whereas the value of the second is incalculable. The missing link lies somewhere in the science of Communication Theory. Communication Theory has developed to become Information Theory. However "information" is not defined by truth/validity; it is defined by probability. If you offer me a service and I respond with "Thank you" my response has a low information content because it is highly probable. If I respond with "спасибо" it has much higher information content because it is less probable (though the meaning is identical if I am Russian!). I am trying to argue that somehow or other Information Theory has to advance to become Knowledge Theory; and by "Knowledge" I mean a Theory which places a value on the meaning (rather than the probability) of the message; and by "value" I mean a term which can be expressed as energy.

You remember my question earlier on: "how can I demonstrate the reality of thoughts without a thinker"? It should now be clear that Knowledge is itself my proof of the reality of thoughts without a thinker. The laws of Physics are a description of how matter behaves. The laws reflect matter. The laws depend on matter. The laws do not depend on sentient beings for anything other than their discovery. Of course I am not arguing that scientific Knowledge exists before it is discovered in the way in which a continent exists before it is discovered. Knowledge about the laws of matter and energy have accreted from thousands of acts of discovery, bit by bit, over centuries. To date only humans have been capable of generating these discoveries. However, though the second law was discovered by humans, it does not depend upon humans for its validity. Knowledge (science) has quite other forms of validation (a digression for this essay). Though discovery is (has been) dependent on humans; once discovered Knowledge has an independent existence and validity which is not rooted in the thinker. Though the thinker gives rise to the thought, the thought can continue without the thinker. And, once Knowledge accretes, no single thinker is capable of knowing all there is to know. So back to my original question: "Where do thoughts hide when they are not being thought?" Answer: "In energy!"

In a curious way I have been suggesting the opposite of a biblical interpretation of the universe. Instead of a Supreme Being creating the heavens and the earth, Adam and Eve, good and evil, and Knowledge; I am arguing that in the beginning was matter and energy, and that matter and energy created life, life created humans, and humans created Knowledge. I am suggesting that Knowledge is the most powerful form of energy, and that it is capable of progression with or without further dependence on humans. Another way of expressing this is: God did not create the universe; the universe is struggling to become God.

Consciousness – The Metamorphosis of a Concept

by

Jacques Naoum

One person asks: what comes next? The other: is it right? Thus differs the Lord from the servant (Kleist)

Consciousness claims a large space in both the sacral and profane realms. It can be defined as the reflection and projection of peoples and nations in their everyday lives. In a religious and ethical context, 'Conscience' serves to protect humanity from its own excesses and demise. As it says in Psalm 91,

> *"The Lord shall give his angels charge over thee, to keep thee in all thy ways. They shall bear thee up in their hands, lest thou dash thy foot against a stone".*

In a secular context, 'Consciousness' can be interpreted as prudence – prudence as a prerequisite for human existence and as a reflection of every human relationship.

But prudence must also be exerted to curb excesses, such as egotism, fanaticism or demagogy, which were inflicted on Western society in the 20th century. They are still disturbingly inching towards satisfaction and tolerance today as the disciples of a merciless "Unconscious" that strives for the Whole, as foreseen by Hegel in the 'Phenomenology of the Spirit'. The striking contradiction between prudence and excess now exists in many areas of the Middle East, for example Lebanon, where about 18 different denominations live in constant strife and yet, in spite of bloodshed and eruptions of violence, they ultimately always return to the nationalist principle of بحيث لا يموت الراعي ولا يهلك رعيته or phonetically "La yamout aray wa la tamout alnazat," or in translation, "So that the shepherd does not die and his flock does not perish." It is a difficult balancing act that is seldom secured even in the Land of the Cedars. It has, however, been the last resort in saving the country from its ultimate doom for centuries – through a unique model of coexistence unparalleled in the entire region which otherwise continues to spread its excesses and misery. So believers and nonbelievers alike combine consciousness and conscience through exile from the paradise of their homeland.

In the religious sense, this takes the form of a rebellion against God's will – Adam seeking the Tree of Knowledge – and in this way, instead of the Old Testament resolution of symbiosis with the Creator (The Tree of Life), being exiled to the land of original sin.

For the age of enlightenment, this takes the form of a relationship between thought and the thinker. In the works of Marx, Hegel and others from the 19th century onwards, this transmission takes place from one state to another within a dialectical process whose goal is synthesis. Here, the truly emancipated human asserts unrestrained dominance over the entire world. Whether it is Hegel's "beautiful soul" or Marx's "classless society," both imply that the world will be overtaken at the end of time. Ultimately, it stands in agreement with the ethical statements of the three largest monotheistic religions: Judaism, Christianity and Islam, whose goals are to lead humanity back to the lost paradise.

Wars, radical changes and revolutions from the beginning of the 19th century effected a certain sensitivity to the concept of consciousness, which has occupied a central place in the nature of Western humanity ever since.

Earlier Descartes adopted the first non-religiously bound concept of consciousness in his famous phrase "Cogito ergo sum" – "I think, therefore I am." This is a qualitative emancipation of an understanding of consciousness tied exclusively to actions. Instead, consciousness is experienced as a kind of human reflection.

This trend in 17th century French enlightenment can be also be felt in the work of Pascal, Descartes' contemporary, particularly Pascal's celebrated maxim, "L'homme n'est ni ange ni bête et qui veut faire l'ange fait la bête." "Man is neither angel nor brute, and he who would act the angel acts the brute." An important approach which remains valid, Pascal's awareness is detached from its moral religious connection and becomes a reflection of human existence. In every era, the exploration of individual consciousness blossoms in different disciplines such as psychology or sensory perception. Further details are beyond the scope of this essay.

The European spiritual history of the 19th and 20th centuries is concerned with this secular, individual or collective career of the newly defined consciousness. Even before Marx said that "being determines consciousness," great thinkers made the issue their own. One of these great thinkers was Hegel, who prioritized the concept of consciousness in his aforementioned work "Phenomenology of the Spirit."

A bevy of lesser-known German and European philosophers have also contributed to the concept of consciousness in various ways, one example of which Treitschke. During their confrontations that culminated only in the waters of national emancipation, Hegel and Marx succeeded in further developing this concept. For them, consciousness was not the goal, but rather the path to the goal.

World history is heading for a climax which will mean the total emancipation of humanity from the state and conventions.

Whether it is Hegel's blessed beautiful soul - or Marx's classless society, both claimed the true human-engineered transformation of a utopian human paradise. Nietzsche also chimes with this division in his work "Also sprach Zarathustra" in which he shaped the physiology of his new superhumans.

These central works, however, favored the individual, and thus begat the biggest catastrophes outside of psychology and parapsychology, namely two world wars, and now their present-day mini-imitations in many parts of the world. All would have the goal of reaching this utopian human paradise.

Perhaps we should consider the humble testimony of Voltaire at the end of his novel Candide: "il faut cultiver notre jardin" – "we should tend our own garden" as the optimal status quo, in order to overcome the mistaken concept of consciousness in its various exaggerations and interpretations.

Two Poems

by

Ruth Fainlight

Numinous

by

Ruth Fainlight

The earth is turning on its axis:
all day long I feel the room,
the house, the street, slide slowly
sideways, right not left
clockwise
north to south
east to west:
as dignified as a Cunard liner
keel parting foaming water
released into its element.

Almost impossible to ignore,
once I sense the planet's movement
that unstoppable gyration.
The thought is dizzying.
My fingers
want to dig into the earth
clutch at every pebble
anything solid
not to be spun off
this suddenly unstable surface.

But soon, daily life's routine
and limitations reassert.
Gone, that total
bodily yet
numinous
realisation (soon forgotten)
of the universal rhythm.
Now, once more, the sun moves
obedient from window to window.
The ground is solid under my feet.

The Difference

by

Ruth Fainlight

Hemming with herringbone stitches
(exquisite, almost invisible),
as small and as regular
as if sewn by that woman
who crouched for hours
close to a smoky lantern
to finish embroidering
the princess's wedding gown
before the morning,

I sit on my bed, needle flashing
in probing afternoon sunlight
that slants through the window;
or later, like a kitchen skivvy
chopping parsley fine enough
to garnish an emperor's dish,
realise that for cook or seamstress
the only possible freedom
is to perfect their skill.

Idle thoughts. I can choose
my occupation. Nobody
gives me orders. Although
we share the thrill of
confirmation when craft
becomes art (and gratitude
for that good fortune)
I know the difference:
I can do as I wish.

Index of Artworks

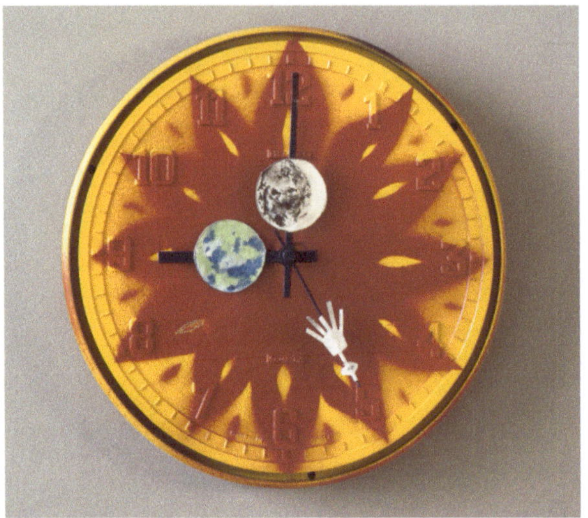

▲ **'Clock'** (1997)
Width x Height x Depth: 22 x 22 x 7 cm
1 Medium; Painted Clock with Collage.
7 Additional Information: From Painted Machines Series.
Artist's Collection

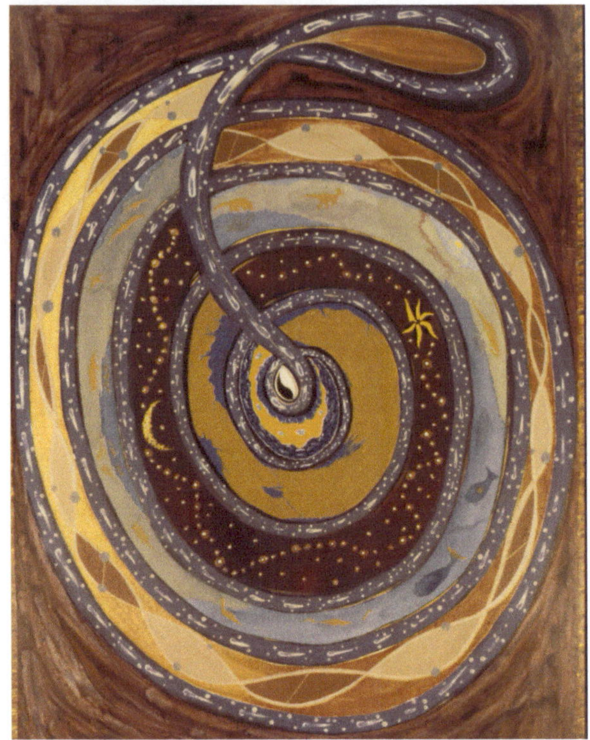

▲ **'Seven Days'** (1991)
Width x Height , 72 x 90 cm
2 Medium : Mixed media on board
9 Additional Information: From Biblical Series, shown Ben Uri
Gallery & Ozten Zeki Gallery with hand coloured catalogue.
Artist's Collection.

Artwork Index for 'Time is a Texture of Consciousness'

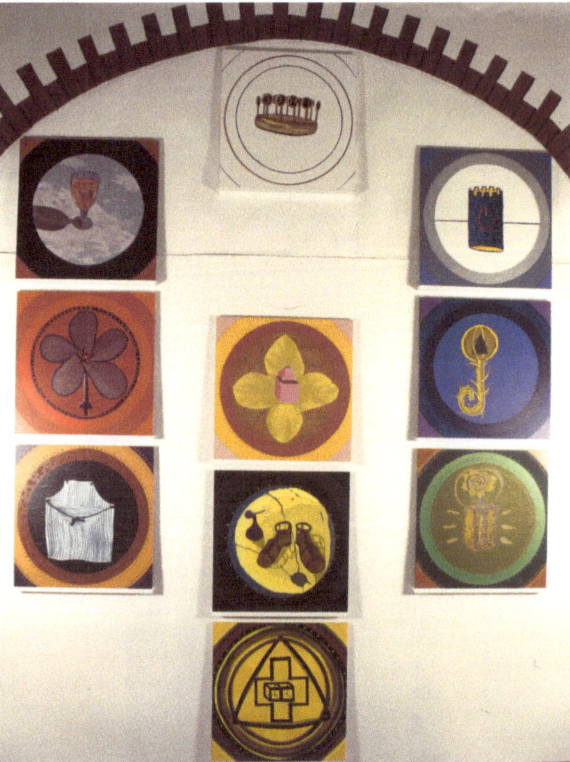

▶ **'Tree of Life' (Kabbalah)** Installation of 10 Paintings (1994)
Width x Height 61 x 61 cm x 10
3 Medium: Oil on Board
11 Additional Information: Bahnhof Westend Show 'Abschied/Arrival'
British Council RCA/DAAD Show in Berlin 1994, and again
in Seigen Public Gallery Germany in 'Dialog' Show, both with
Christine Kühn. This Photo was taken in my London Studio before
packing work. Note painted brick arch.
Central painting 'Schoheit/Beauty' Goldstein Collection Kreuztal,
Germany.
Others 9 in Artist's collection.

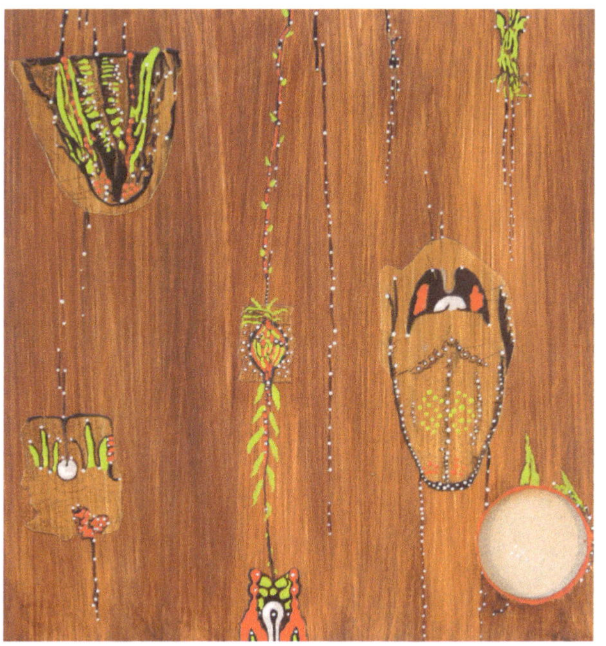

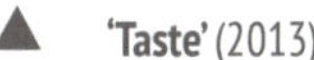

▲ **'Taste'** (2013)
4 Width x Height 29 x 34 cm
Medium: Paint & Collage on Panel.
13 Additional Information; Part of 'Senses' series. Collage from Gray's etched diagrams in his medical textbook Guide to Human Anatomy. Graining techniques from Parry's Graining & Marbling book. Embedding fossil of human body part in a tree. One sign buried in another sign. Artist's Collection.

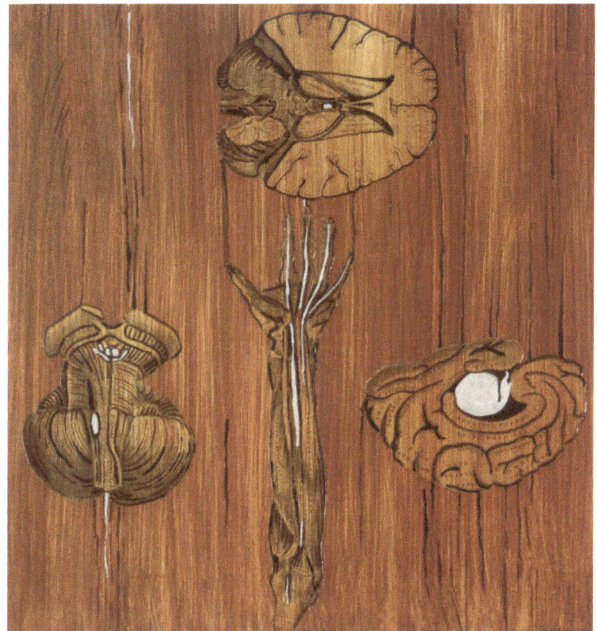

▲ **'Touch'** (2013)
4 Width x Height 29 x 34 cm
Medium: Paint & Collage on Panel.
14 Additional Information: Part of 'Senses' series. Artist's Collection.

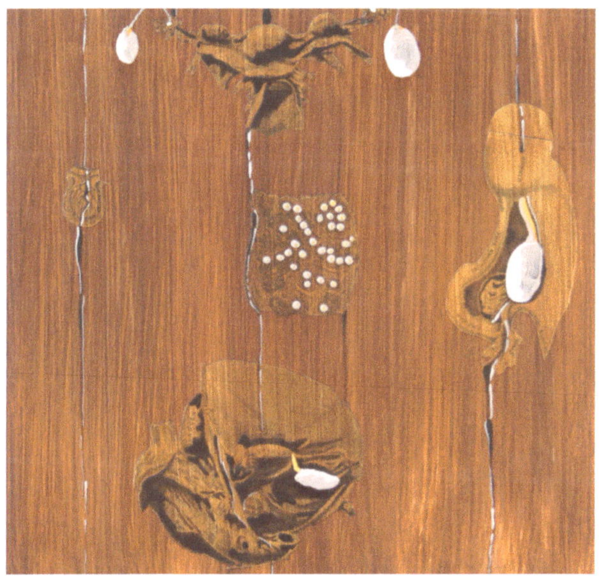

▲ **'Eggs'** (2013)
4 Width x Height 29 x 34 cm.
Medium: Paint & Collage on Panel.
15 Additional Information: Part of 'Senses' series. Artist's Collection.

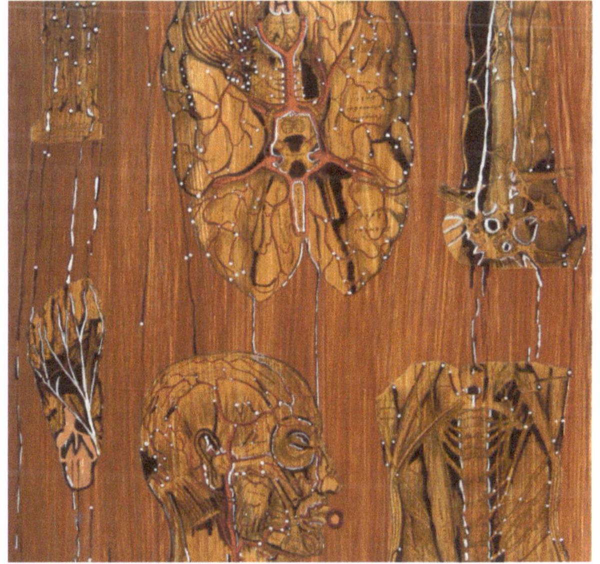

▲ **'Limb Awareness'** (2013)
4 Width x Height 29 x 34 cm
Medium: Paint & Collage on Panel.
16 Additional Information: Part of 'Senses' series. Artist's Collection.

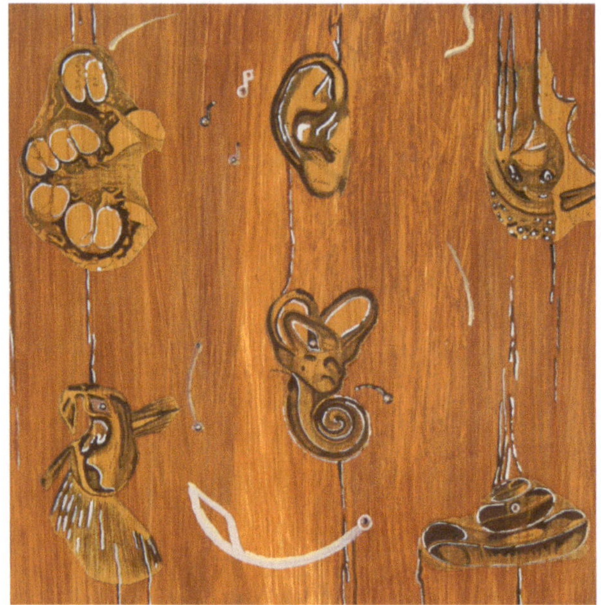

▲ **'Hearing'** (2013)
Width x Height 29 x 34 cm
4 Medium: Paint & Collage on Panel.
17 Additional Information: Part of 'Senses' series. Collage from Gray's etched diagrams in his medical textbook Guide to Human Anatomy. Graining techniques from Parry's Graining & Marbling book. Embedding fossil of human body part in a tree. One sign buried in another sign. Artist's Collection.

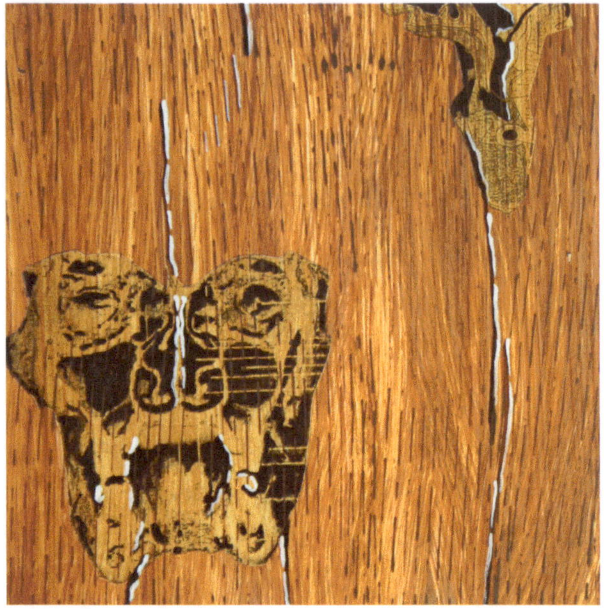

▲ **'Smell'** (2013)
Width x Height 29 x 34 cm
4 Medium: Paint & Collage on Panel.
18 Additional Information: Part of 'Senses' series. Collage from Gray's etched diagrams in his medical textbook Guide to Human Anatomy. Graining techniques from Parry's Graining & Marbling book. Embedding fossil of human body part in a tree. One sign buried in another sign. Artist's Collection.

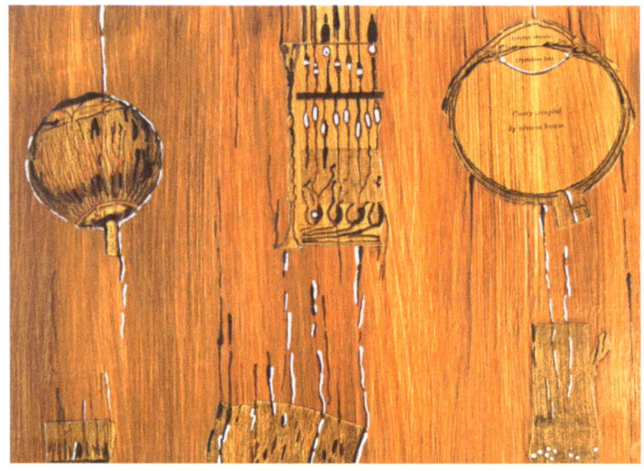

▲ **'Sight'** (2013)
Width x Height 29 x 34 cm
4 Medium: Paint & Collage on Panel.
20 Additional Information: Part of 'Senses' series. Collage from Gray's etched diagrams in his medical textbook Guide to Human Anatomy. Graining techniques from Parry's Graining & Marbling book. Embedding fossil of human body part in a tree. One sign buried in another sign.
Artist's Collection.

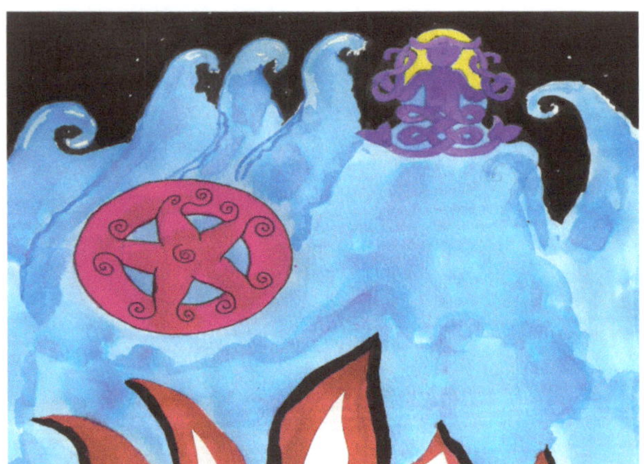

▲ **'The Never Ending Passage of the Soul'** (2015)
Width x Height 21 cm x 29.5 cm
5 Medium: Inks on paper
23 Additional Information; This is a picture done in a day of a painting that took a week in 1988. The original was damaged in storage in a damp basement in the South of France. The photo was taken in haste on a windy but sunlit fire escape from the mural studio of the RCA Painting department when it was in Exhibition Road, and the slide was too out of focus to reproduce in a book. It was an interesting experience trying to revisualise the motifs of the Celtic merman, the five section circle and the fire and water. I changed the title in light of what I think now, and a recent series of paintings but pleased that I was onto it all those years ago. Artist's Collection

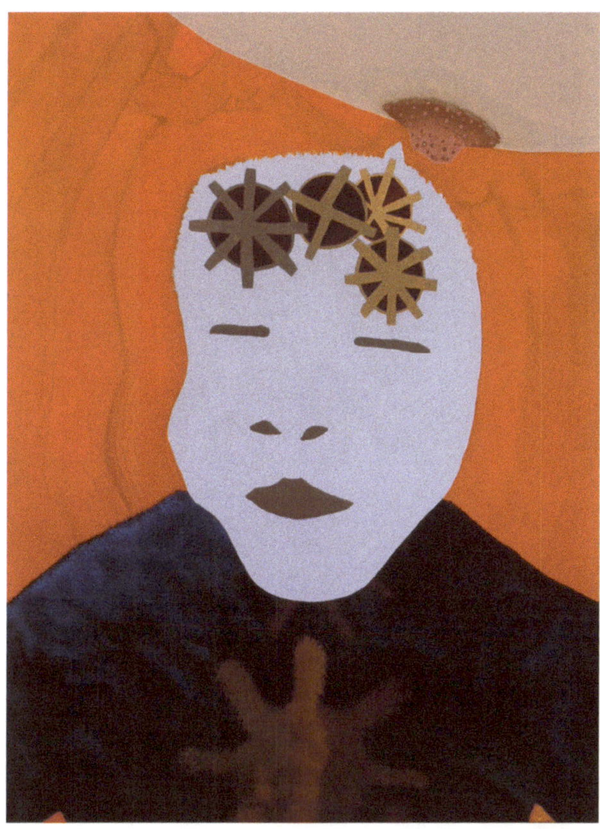

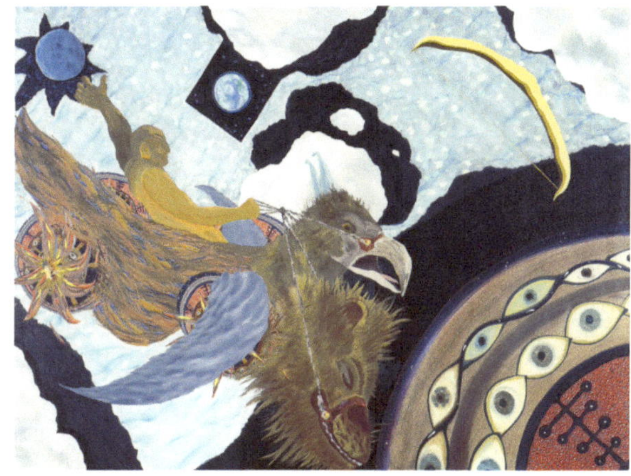

▲ **'Vision of Ezekiel's Chariot'** (1995)
7 Width x Height 131 x 94 cm
Medium: Oil on Canvas.
27 Additional Information. One reality ripped opened to reveal another. Book of Revelations. Artist's collection

◀ **'Dream Machine'** (1997)
6 Width x Height 59 x 76 cm
Medium: Oil on Board
25 Additional Information.
Private Collection, London.

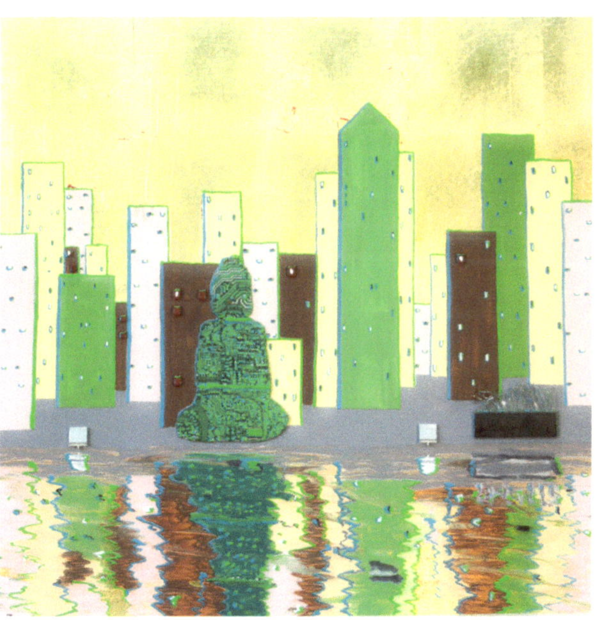

▲ **'Buddha hacks the Internet'** (2013)
9 Width x Height 61 x 61 cm.
Medium : Oil, Circuits & Gold Leaf on Board
31 Additional Information: China Cyber attic items in news. Snowden & Surveillance case. Alchemy, the Internet & Consciousness.
Artist's Collection.

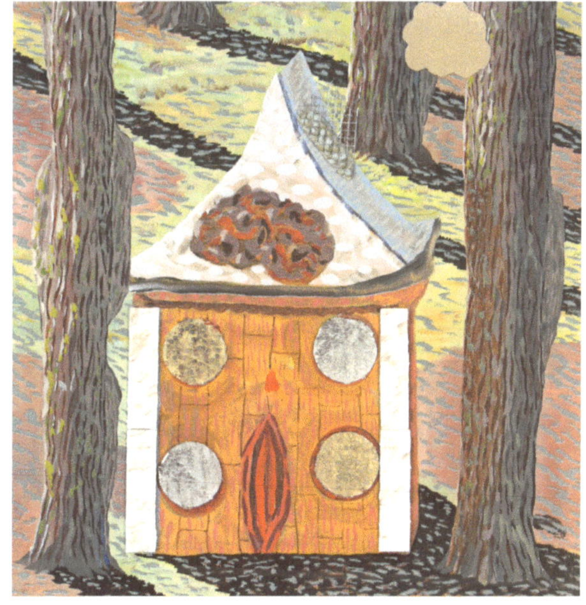

▲ **'Walk in the Woods of The Collective Unconscious'** (2013)
8 Width x Height 51 x 56 cm.
Medium : Oil Paint , Metal, Plastic, Sandpaper, Resin on Board.
29 Additional Information. I stayed near Muir Woods one time.
Artist's Collection.

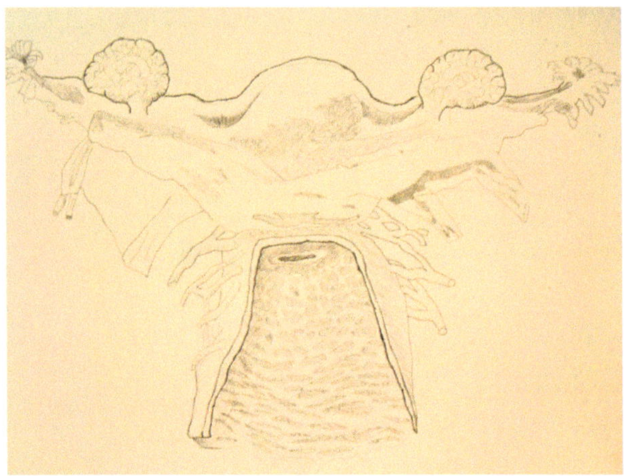

▲ **'Uterus with two Brains'** - Drawing (2013)
10 Width x Height : A3
Medium: Pencil on Paper
33 Additional Information; Part of Senses Painting research. Gray's Anatomy. The title is an Anima take on Steve Martin's film. Artist's collection.

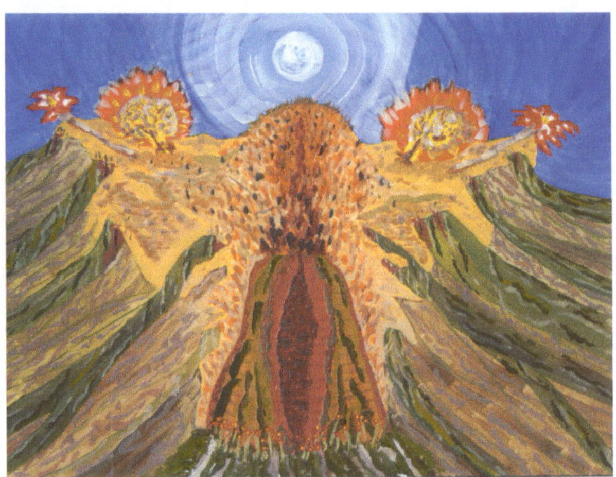

▲ **'Delphi'** (2013)
Width x Height A3
11 Medium: Oil on Board
35 Additional Information. Summer Holiday to Great Mynn in Shropshire that year. Many years ago holiday to Delphi. Both 'Primeval Mother Earth' locations. Based on drawing 'Uterus with two Brains'. Artist's collection.

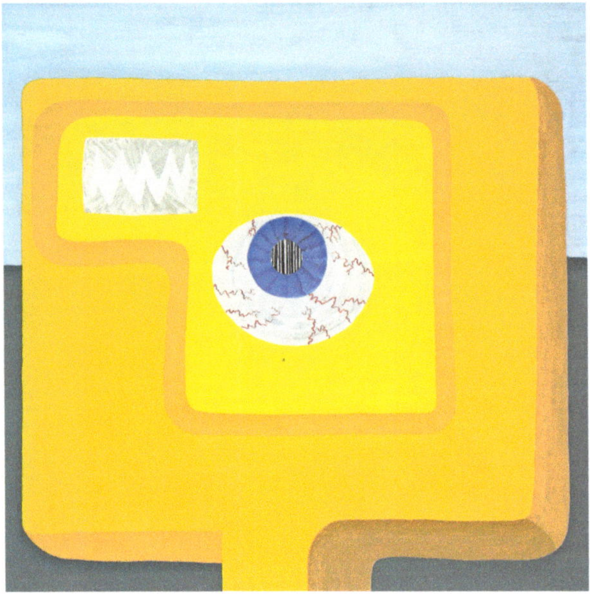

▲ **'Auto self-consciousness'** (2007)
Width x Height 51 x 56 cm.
12 Medium : Oil on Board
39 Additional Information: Previously called 'Car Surveillance', part of Surveillance series from 2007, lots of paintings with eyes in them. London Congestion Charge & CCTV camera increased use. Artist's collection.

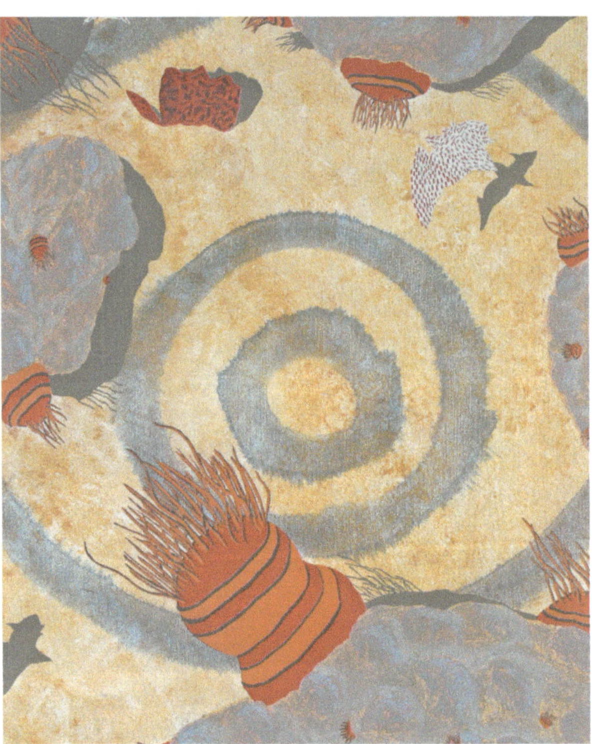

▲ **'Fish Can'** (1996)
Width x Height 66 x 56 cm
13 Medium: Oil on Board
41 Additional Information: Also called 'Tin Can'. Southerndown Beach Wales. Artist's collection.

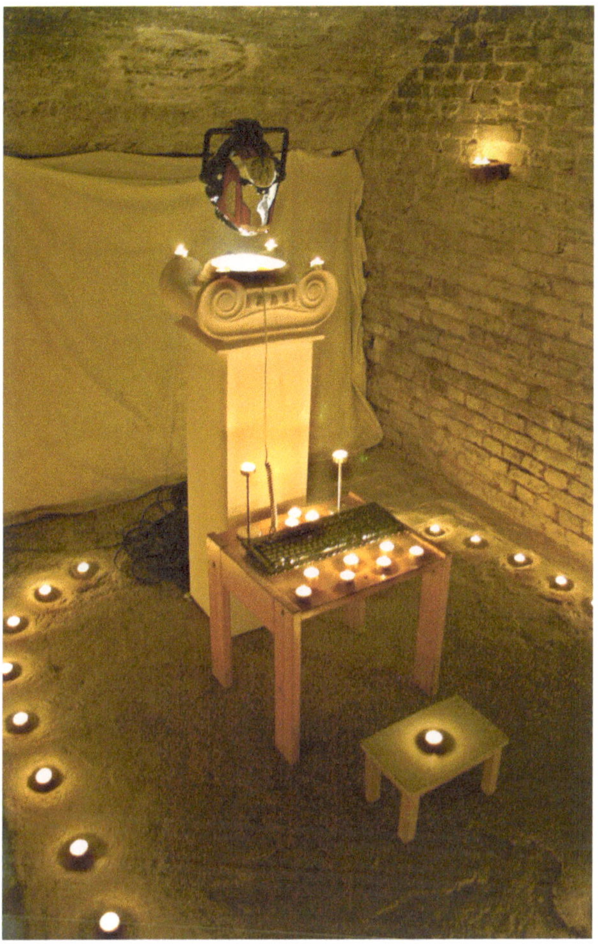

▲ 14 45 **'The Altar of Communication'**
Installation in Weekend Gallery, Berlin (2013)
Width x Height x Depth 3m x 2 m x 3m
Medium: Painted & Collaged Cyberman Helmet, & painted computer keyboard from earlier painted machine series, found classical plinth and tea candles.
Additional Information: That room has a curved ceiling and a memorial shrine in it.
Artist's collection.

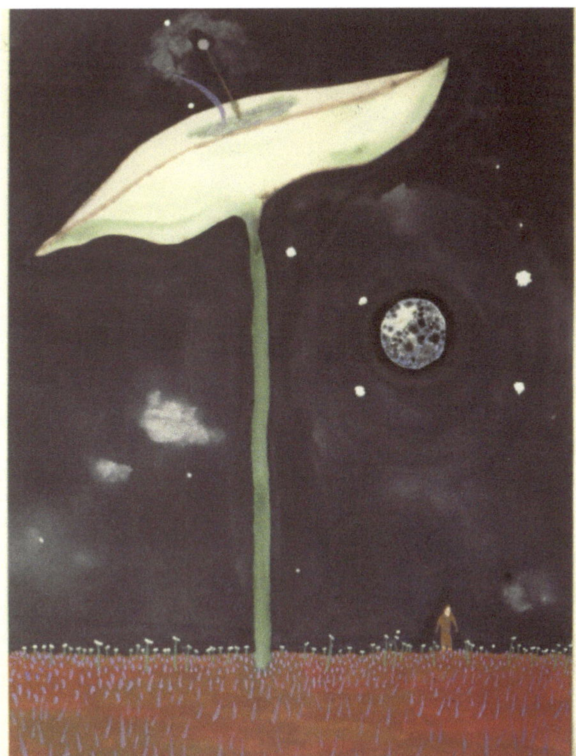

▲ 15 46 **'Wandering St Francis'** (1992)
Width x Height 46 x 61 cm
Medium: Gouache on Paper.
Additional Information; From Painting series on paper based on a book called 'The Little Flowers of St Francis' about the Saint from Assisi and his followers that formed the Franciscan monastic Order. Medieval environmentalist movement. Catalogue for Show. Collection Hordern, London.

▶ 16 47 Hanging Gracie Wallpaper in a reception room in the Boltons, London. (2013)
Additional Information: This is my day job.

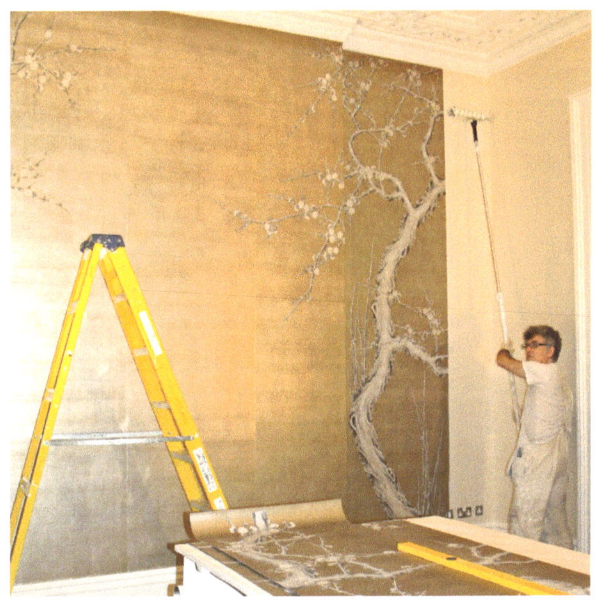

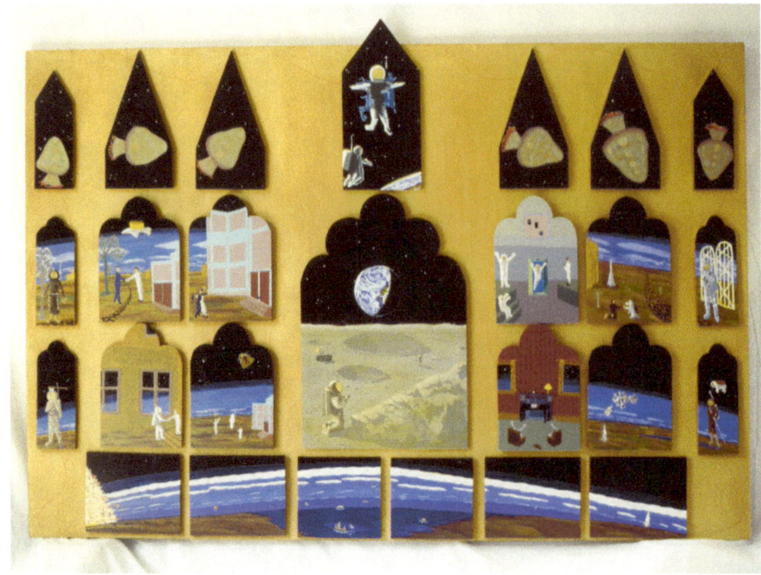

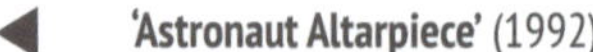

'Astronaut Altarpiece' (1992)
Width x Height: Total Dimension 183 x122 cm
17 Medium: Oil on 26 Panels, mounted on a painted gold canvas stretcher.
51 Additional Information: Whole Altarpiece based on St Francis Altarpiece by Sasestta (Siena 1392-1450) some panels e.g. Wolf of Gubbio in National Gallery London Sainsbury's Wing and Microgallery library database.
'Astronauts floating in Space' (Artist's collection), other pieces in Dr Brian Whitton (Microbiologist Durham) Collection & Author 'Tunnard' (20th C Surrealist). This connection led to the show 'Androids, Robots & Golems' at Trevelyan College, Durham University 1998 with Catalogue (Meshoulam/Weiner/Reid).
The Astronaut Altarpiece replaces Medieval Saints with Astronauts, the Desert wilderness becomes Outer Space, The Virgin Mary becomes Planet Earth. I was reading Marina Warner's Book "Alone of all her sex' at the time. Watching the moon landing on TV was a huge shift in human consciousness.

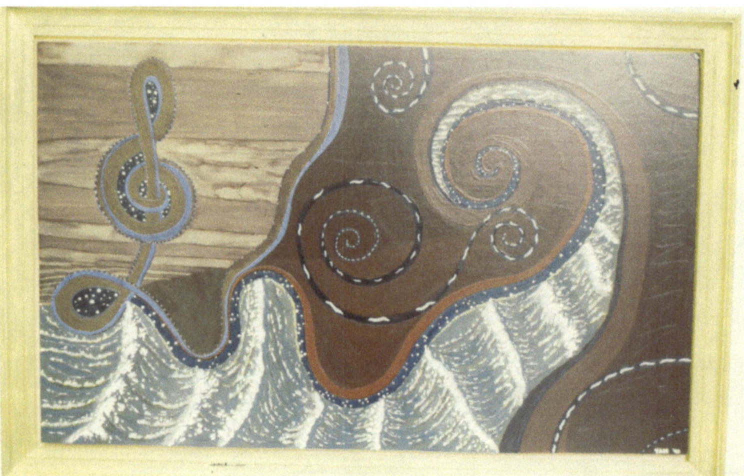

'Soundwave' (1990)
Width x Height 67 x 40 plus painted frame
18 Medium: Oil on Board
Additional Information: Part of 'Music' series.

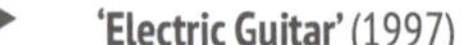

'Electric Guitar' (1997)
Width x Height 61 x 60 cm
19 Medium: Oil on Panel
53 Additional Information: This is a portrait one of my favourite Semi Acoustic guitars.
Private Collection, London.

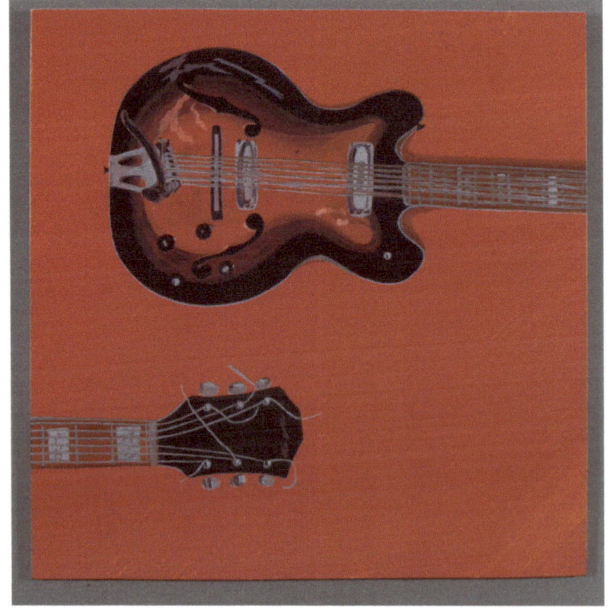

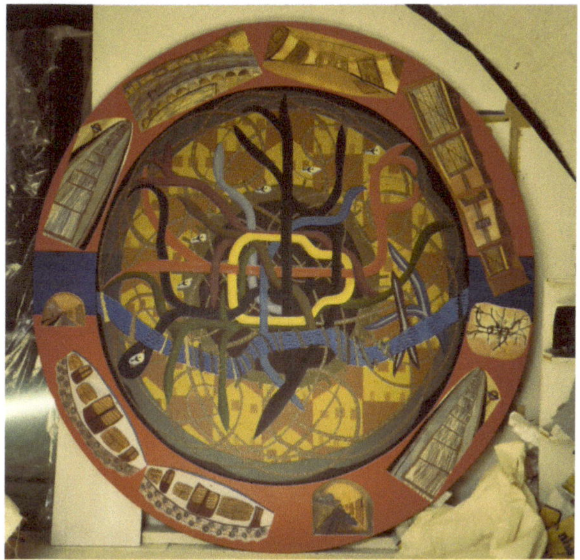

▲ 20 55
'Journey' (1990)
Width x Height: Circular Total Diameter 220 cm
Medium: Central Circular Painting Oil on Canvas. Outer rim painted panel with collaged acrylic on paper paintings.
Additional Information: This painting is all about the structure of London, its zones and travel connections under and over land and water. It is photographed where I painted it in London Bridge Studios in a Railway Arch in Bermondsey. The trains used to rattle overhead.
Private Collection, Brighton.

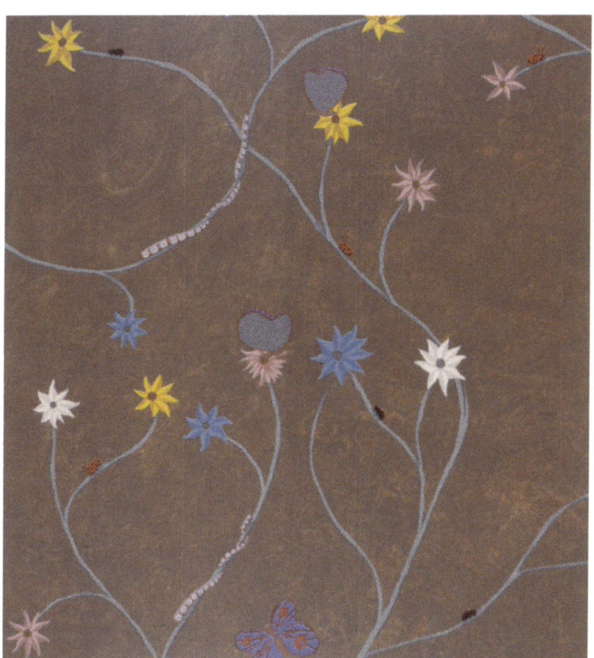

▲ 21 57
'London Garden' (2002)
Width x Height 51 x61 cm
Medium: Oil on Panel.
Additional Information: The layout is based on a German gelatine print floral wallpaper and textile pattern. The insects are little transport machines, a tube train caterpillar, a ladybird double decker bus, a black beetle taxi.
Private Collection San Francisco.

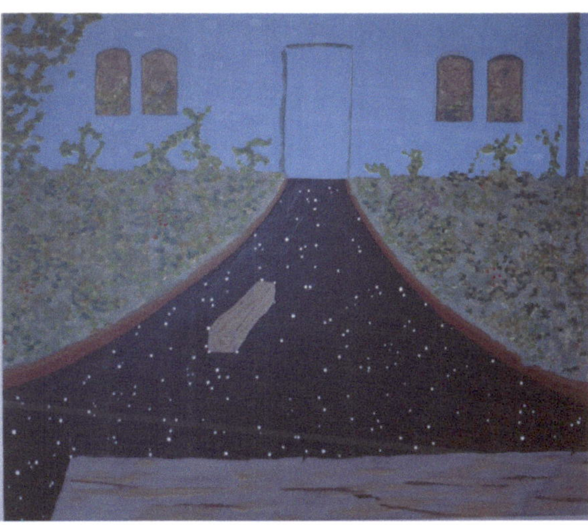

▲ 22 59
'Stars on the Ground' (2001)
Width x Height 60 x 51 cm
Medium: Oil on Panel
Additional Information: Based on our garden in Brixton. The ground becomes outer space, one space is ripped open to imagine another beyond.

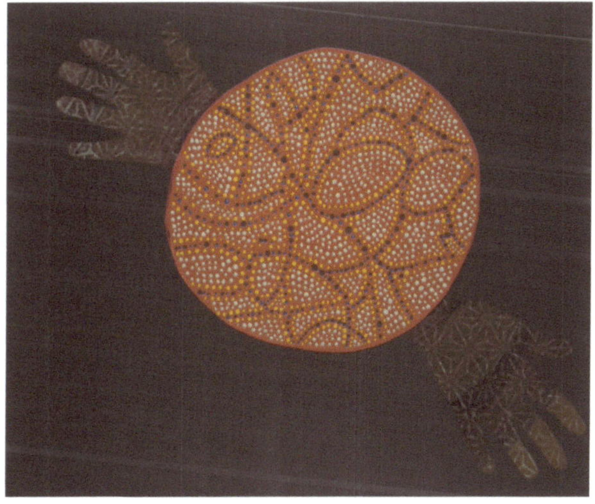

▲ 23 61
'Universe with Two Hands' (1999)
Width x Height 61 x 66 cm
Medium: Oil on Panel
Additional Information. Part of Macro-Micro series. The first Hubble telescope photos had recently been published.

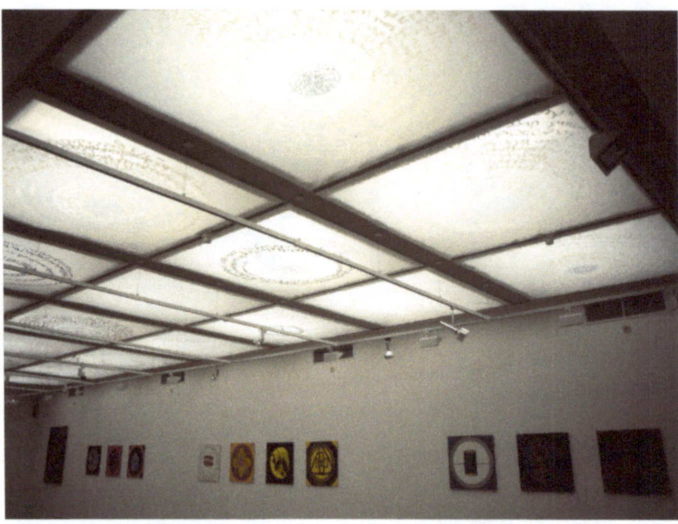

◀ **Installation / Painting Show 'Dialog' with Christine Kühn in Seigen Public Gallery,**
24 Germany (1996)
63 Width x Height
Medium: Ceiling suspended Transparent Paintings, paint on plastic. Wall hung Paintings Oil on Panel and canvas. Kabbalah related work (Tree of Life 10 Sefirot series, Ezekiel's chariot, Diagrams of Splendour (Zohar) and some space-time diagram abstract paintings).
Additional Information: Exploration of the presence of text and image.
'Schoheit/Beauty' Goldstein Collection, Kreuztal, Germany. Others in Artists collections.

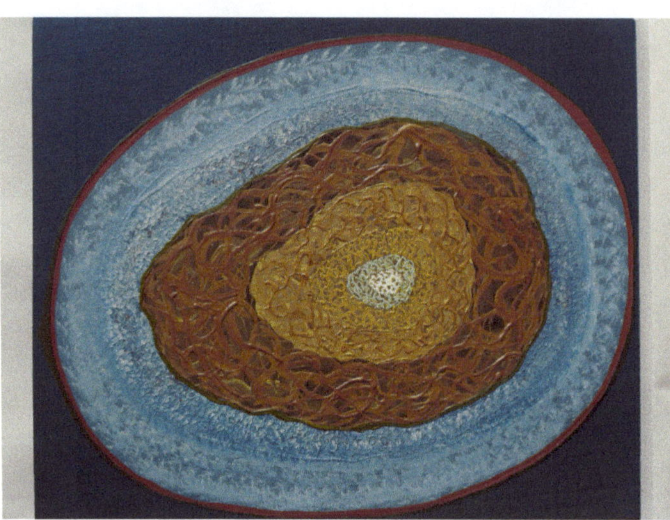

▲ **'Universe, Shell and Kernel'** (1993)
Width x Height 34 x42 cm
25 Medium: Oil on Panel
65 Additional Information: From 'Zohar-Diagrams of Splendour' series of 34 paintings. G. Scholem's translation of each chapter written out by hand on reverse of each painting. Exhibited in "As Above, so below' two person show with Herve Constant Ben Uri Gallery, Dean St, Soho, London. 1995.
Here the Universe is shown as a brain inside a nut, a diagram of consciousness. Private Collection, London UK

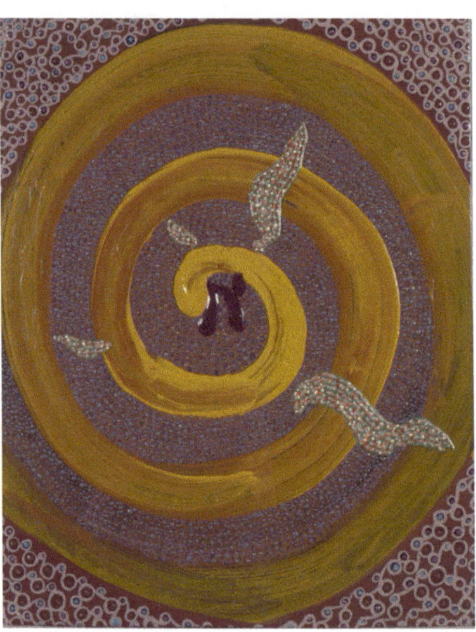

▲ **'The Beginning'** (1993)
Width x Height 34 x 42 cm
27 Medium: Oil on Panel
69 Additional Information: From 'Zohar-Diagrams of Splendour' series of 34 paintings. G. Scholem's translation of each chapter written out by hand on reverse of each painting. Exhibited in "As Above, so below' two person show with Herve Constant Ben Uri Gallery, Dean St, Soho, London. 1995. Here the beginning of the cycle of the Universe is shown as the first letter of language (The N shape is Aleph in Hebrew, or Alpha if it were Greek, or A if it were English) forming, as all energy and matter is released. This is a diagram of consciousness beginning with language. "In the beginning was the word". The dots of Aboriginal painting, are the space and time travelling map points in a walkabout journey. Private Collection, London UK

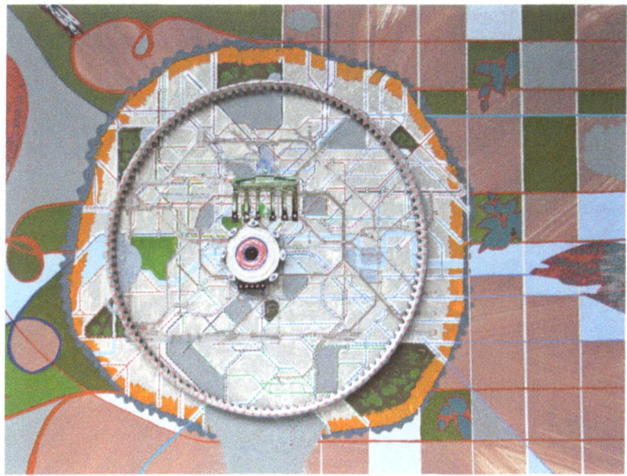

▲ **'Berlin – London Brain Map'** 2014.
Width x Height 61 by 51cm
26 Medium: Mixed media on board
67 Additional Information: Transport maps of London and Berlin mixed together. Brandenburg Gate and London Eye. Wheel rim, replaced parts from my van engine. All in a head where one side of the brain sets out information in a grid, the other side in organic curves. The city as a manifestation of the mind.

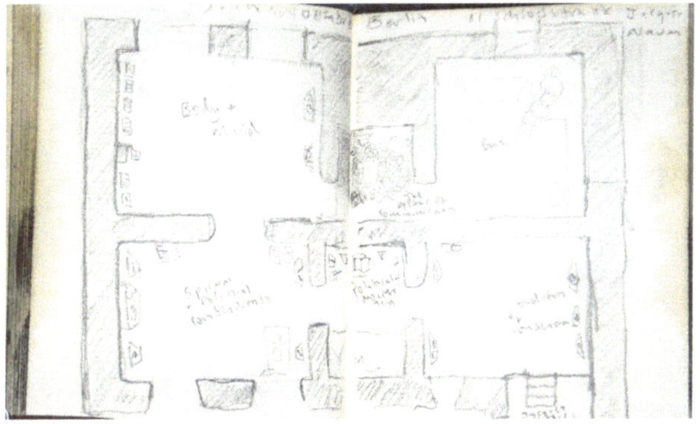

▲ **Sketchbook plan, Drawing Diagram/ Map of Show Installation** (2013)
28 Width x Height 19 x 13 cm
Medium: Pencil on Paper
Additional Information: This is the drawing showing the layout of the show at the Weekend Gallery, Berlin.

▶ **'What is Murdoch up to?'** (2009-11)
Width x Height 60 x 70 cm
30 Medium: Collage & Paint on Board.
Additional Information; From a Series of Collages. Photos taken on Four Horses of The Apocalypse Demonstration (Kettled in front of Bank of England, London) at beginning of most recent Financial Crash. Collaged bank notes from Performance piece with Steven Levon Ounanian at Shunt art club under London Bridge Station. Eye from adapted US Dollar. Also collage section of reproduced Durer woodblock cut. Hacking scandal news breaking. Finance, politics, police, media combination. Artist's collection.

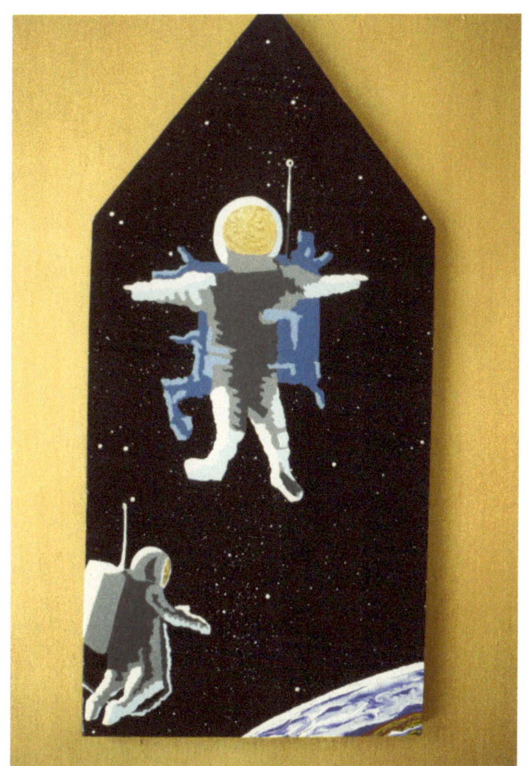

▲ **'Astronauts floating in Space'** (1992)
Width x Height: 42 x 20 cm
29 Medium: Oil on Panel.
Additional Information: Central top pinnacle panel from 'Astronaut Altarpiece' Width x Height .Total size 122 x 183 cm comprising 26 panels based on St Francis Altarpiece by Sasestta (Siena 1392-1450) some panels e.g. Wolf of Gubbio in National Gallery London Sainsbury's Wing and Microgallery library database. 'Astronauts floating in Space' (Artist's collection) other pieces in Dr Brian Whitton (Microbiologist Durham) Collection & Author 'Tunnard' (20th Century British Surrealist).

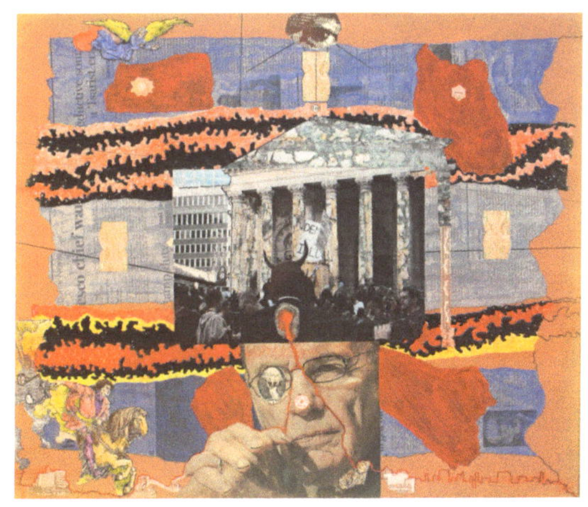

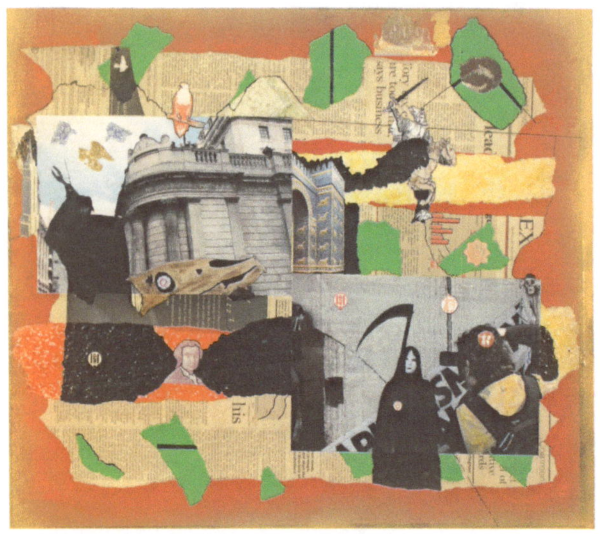

31 **'The Four Horses of the Apocalypse open a Joint Bank Account'** (2009-11)
Width x Height 60 x 70 cm
Medium: Collage & Paint on Board.
Additional Information; From a Series of Collages. Photos taken on Four Horses of The Apocalypse Demonstration (Kettled in front of Bank of England, London) at beginning of most recent Financial Crash. Here a large puppet of Death with a Sickle on a Horse passes by the Bank of England while police and/or press take photos of demonstrators from the balcony. Collaged bank notes from Performance piece with Steven Levon Ounanian at Shunt art club under London Bridge Station. Eye from US Dollar. Also collage section of reproduced Durer woodblock cut. Hacking scandal news breaking. Finance, politics, police, media combination.
Artist's collection.

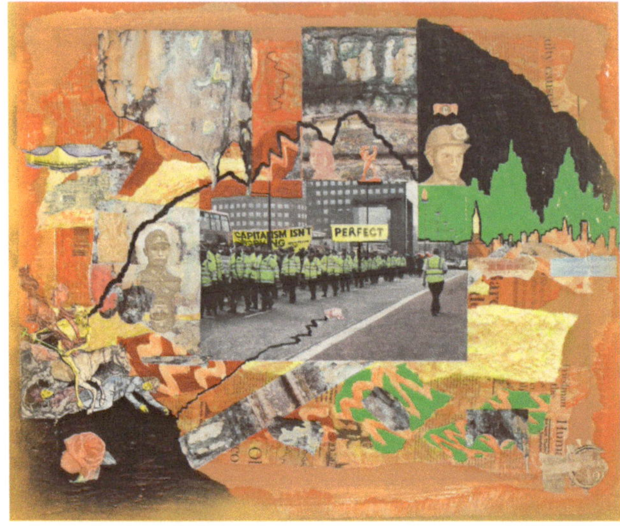

32 **'Capitalism isn't Perfect'** (2009-11)
Width x Height 60 x 70 cm
Medium: Collage & Paint on Board
Additional Information; From a Series of Collages. Photos taken on Four Horses of The Apocalypse Demonstration (Kettled in front of Bank of England, London) at beginning of most recent Financial Crash. Here some demonstrators hold banner which I have changed from 'Capitalism isn't Working' (in itself changed from 1979 election poster 'Labour isn't Working') to 'Capitalism isn't Perfect'. Collaged bank notes ('Heroic' images from the old East European Block, or Military Rulers from the Far East) from Performance piece with Steven Levon Ounanian at Shunt art club under London Bridge Station. Eye from US Dollar. Also collage section of reproduced Durer woodblock cut prints. Hacking scandal news breaking. Finance, politics, police, media combination.
Artist's collection.

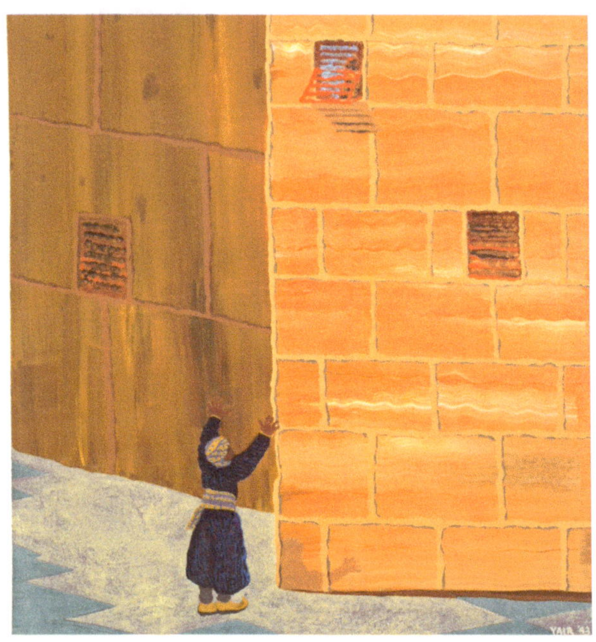

33 **'Lovers of the Torah'** (1993)
Width x Height 34 x 42 cm
Medium: Oil on Board
Additional Information: From 'Diagrams of Splendour' Series 34 paintings from 34 chapters of 'Zohar – Book of Splendour' (G.Scholem translation of Jewish Kabbalah Mystic Text). Chapter copied out by hand on the back of the painting .
Collection Dr Pantke, Berlin.

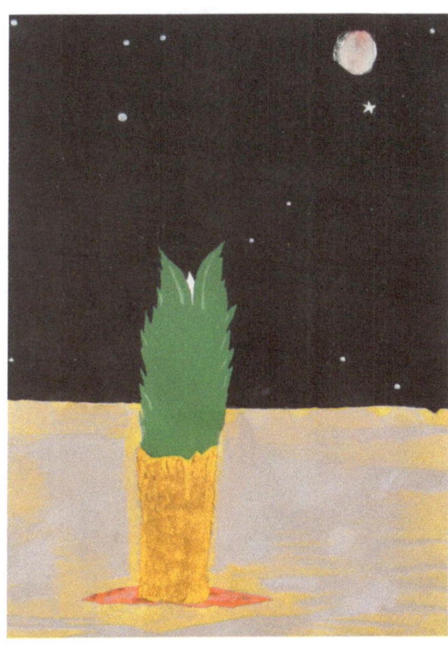

▲ **'Birth of the Star of Hope.'** (1) (2012)
Width x Height: 32 x 42 cm
34 Medium: Acrylic paint on Arches Paper
Additional Information: Set of six paintings on paper for two person show called 'Arab Spring' with Jad Salman at the Weekend Gallery, Berlin 2012. Artist's collection.

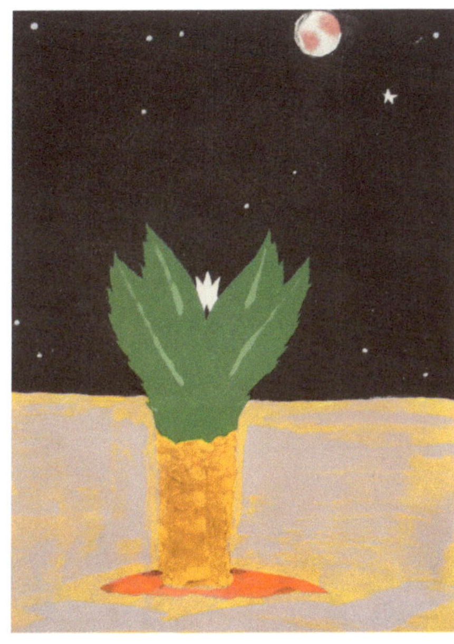

▲ **'Birth of the Star of Hope.'** (2)
Width x Height: 32 x 42 cm
Medium: Acrylic paint on Arches Paper

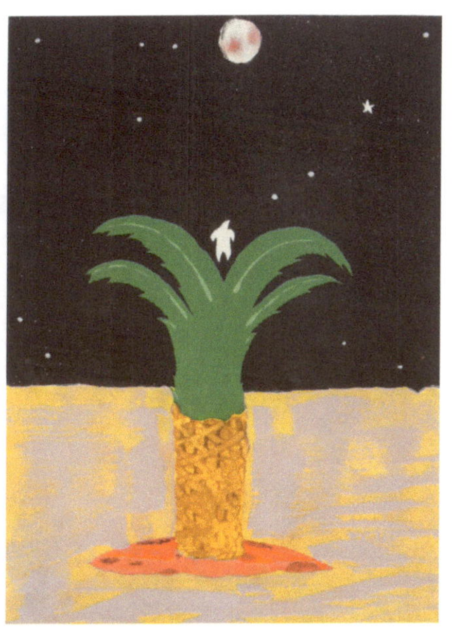

▲ **'Birth of the Star of Hope.'** (3) (2012)
Width x Height: 32 x 42 cm
Medium: Acrylic paint on Arches Paper

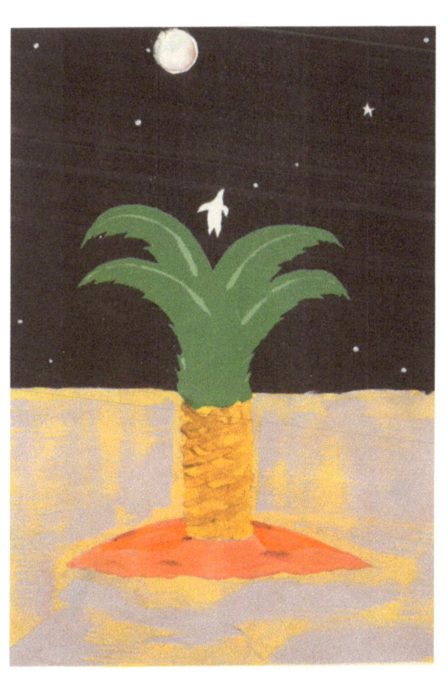

▲ **'Birth of the Star of Hope.'** (4) (2012)
Width x Height: 32 x 42 cm
Medium: Acrylic paint on Arches Paper

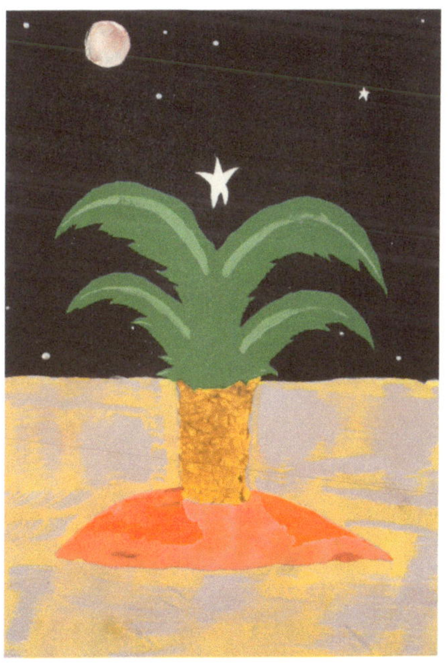

▲ **'Birth of the Star of Hope.'** (5) (2012)
Width x Height: 32 x 42 cm
Medium: Acrylic paint on Arches Paper

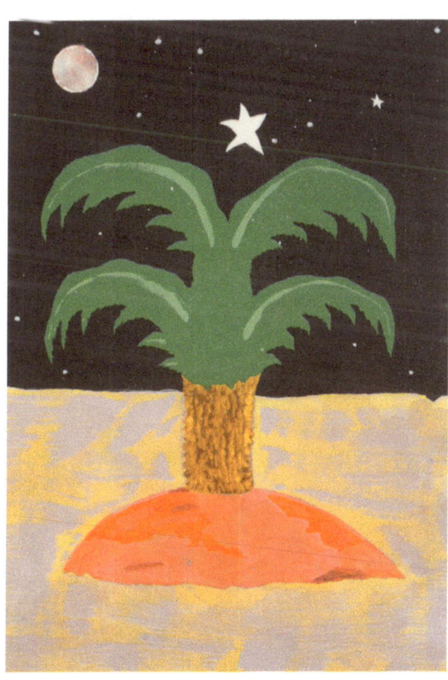

▲ **'Birth of the Star of Hope.'** (6) (2012)
Width x Height: 32 x 42 cm
Medium: Acrylic paint on Arches Paper

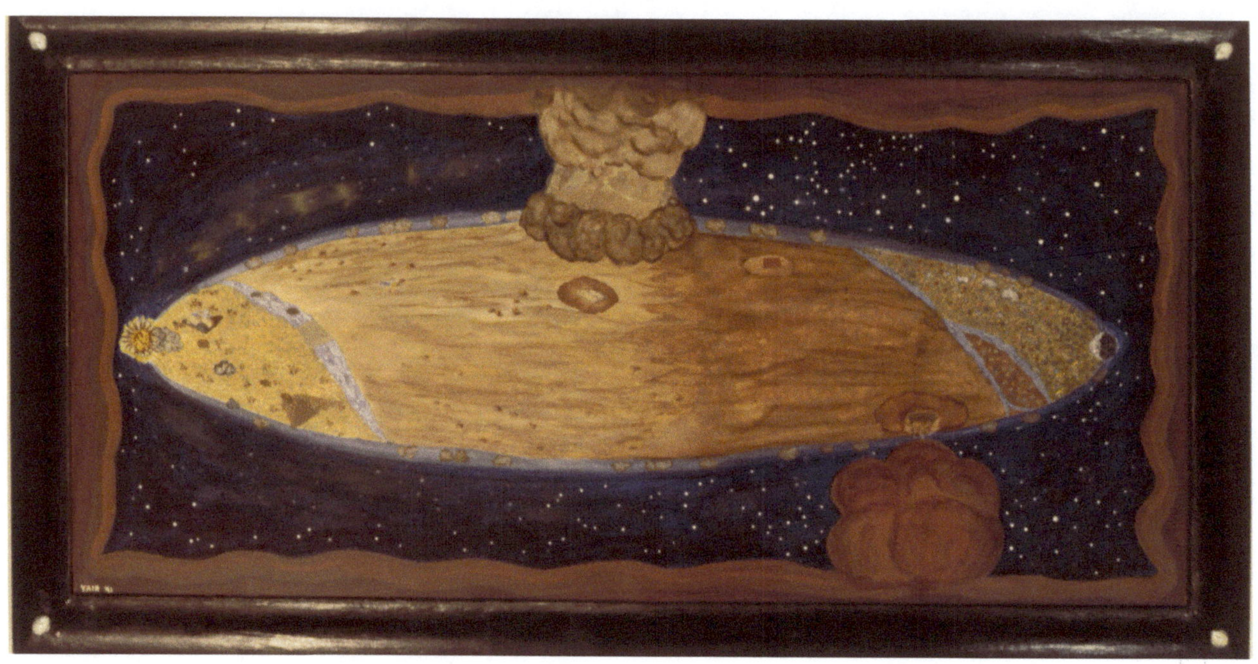

▲ **'Exodus'** (1991)
35 Width x Height 92 x 50 cm
Medium; Oil on Board
Additional Information: From Biblical Series Ozten Zeki Gallery Show with Hand Printed/Painted Catalogue.
Decorated Frame.
Collection Barry, London.

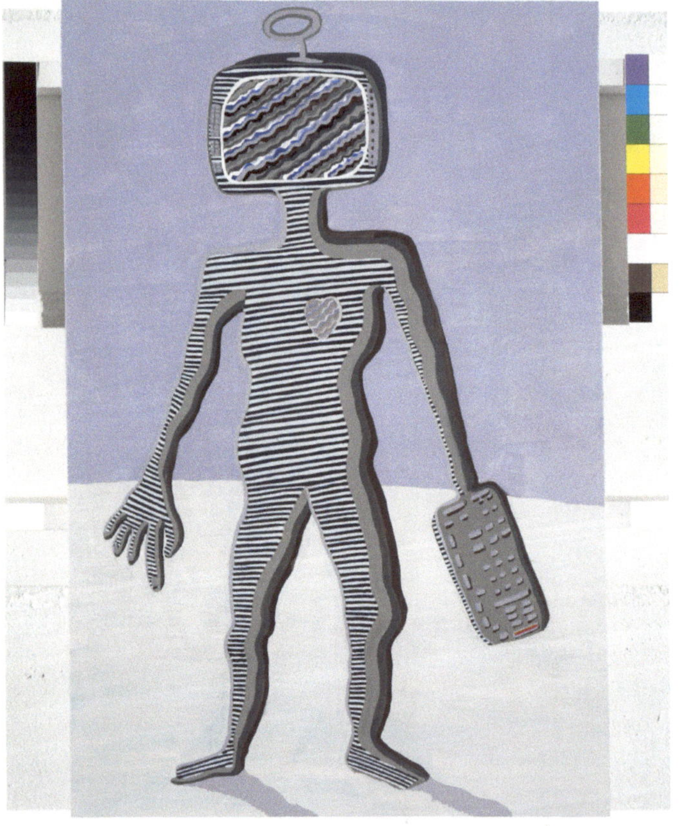

◀ **'T.V. Android'** (1996)
36 Width x Height 42 x 61cm
Medium: Oil on Board.
Additional Information: From Series 'Androids, Robots and Golems' Show at Durham University 1998 with Catalogue (Meshoulam/Weiner/Reid).
Artist's Collection.

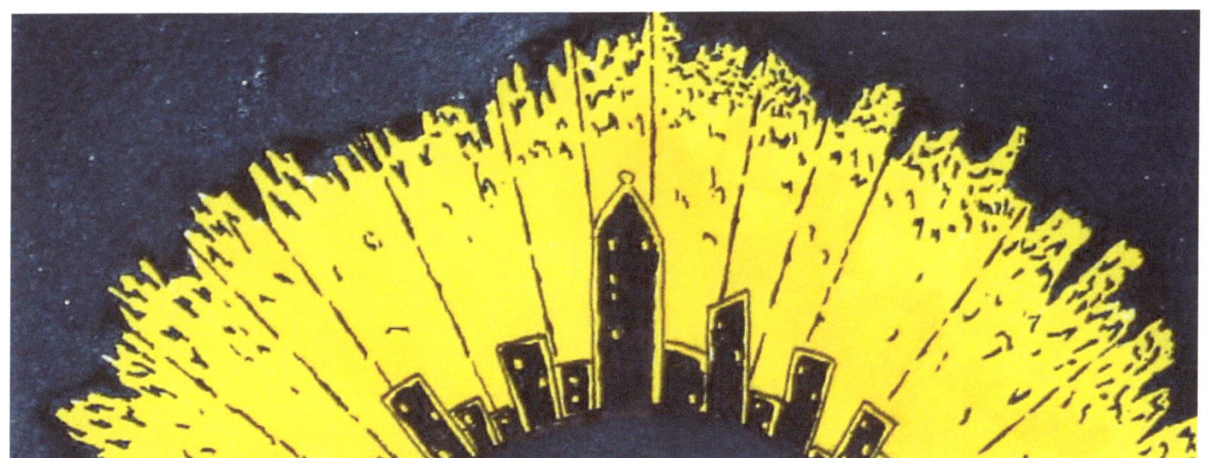

‘Vinyl Cities and other Stories’

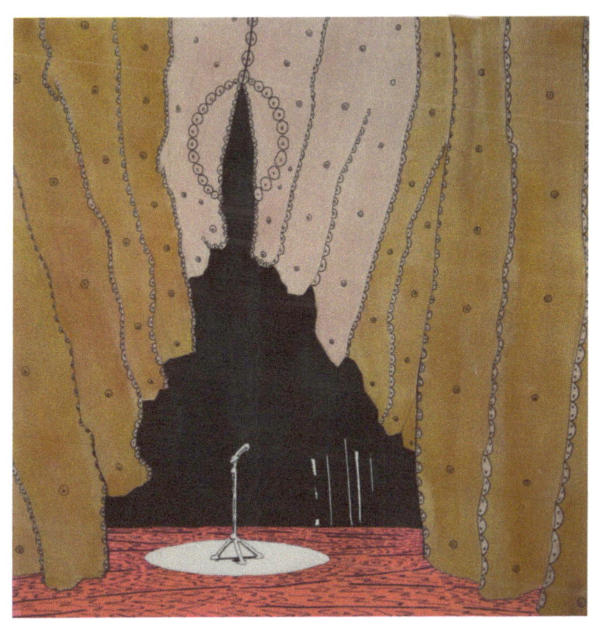

▲ 1 **As the gig ended**
Width x Height x Depth: 30 x 30 cm
Medium; Inks on Paper.
Additional Information: From 'Vinyl Cities and other Stories Exhibition'. Collection Jo & Jim

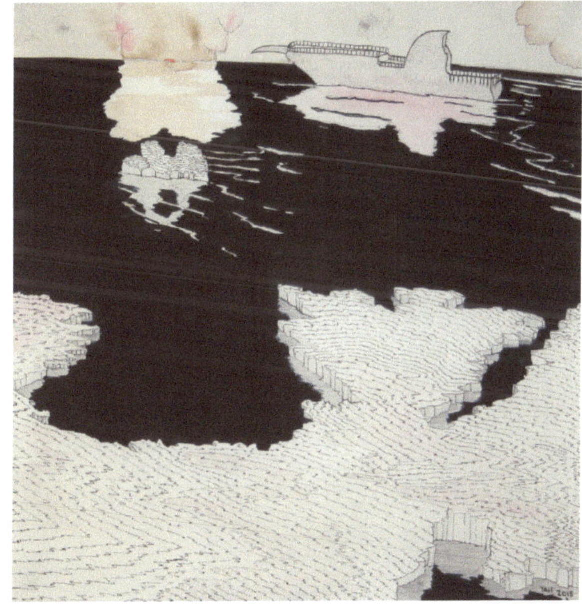

▲ 2 **another chunk of vinyl melted.**
Width x Height x Depth: 30 x 30 cm
Medium; Inks on Paper.
Additional Information: From 'Vinyl Cities and other Stories Exhibition'.

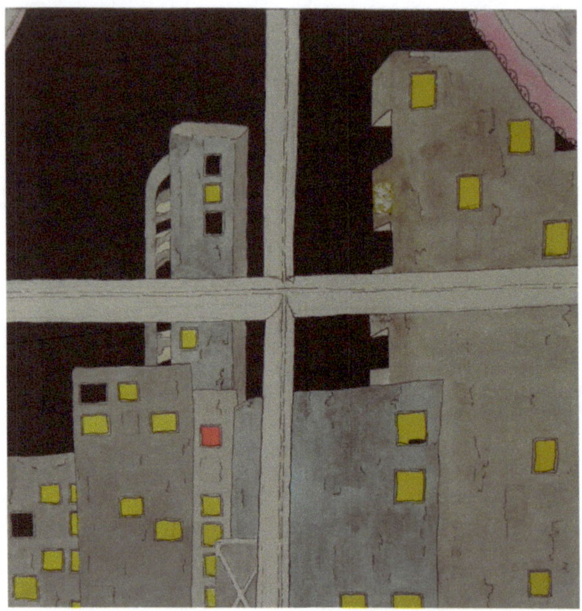

▲ 3 **It seemed like a quiet evening in this city.**
Width x Height x Depth: 30 x 30 cm
Medium; Inks on Paper.
Additional Information: From 'Vinyl Cities and other Stories Exhibition'. Artist Collection

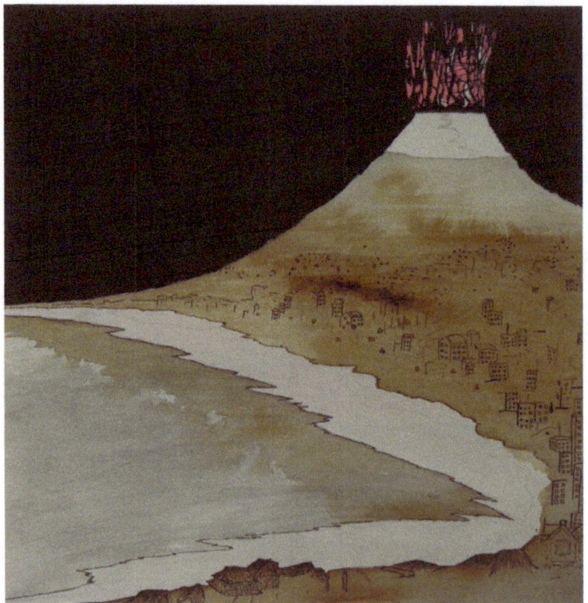

▲ 4 **But around the world some things began to move**
Width x Height x Depth: 30 x 30 cm
Medium; Inks on Paper.
Additional Information: From 'Vinyl Cities and other Stories Exhibition'.

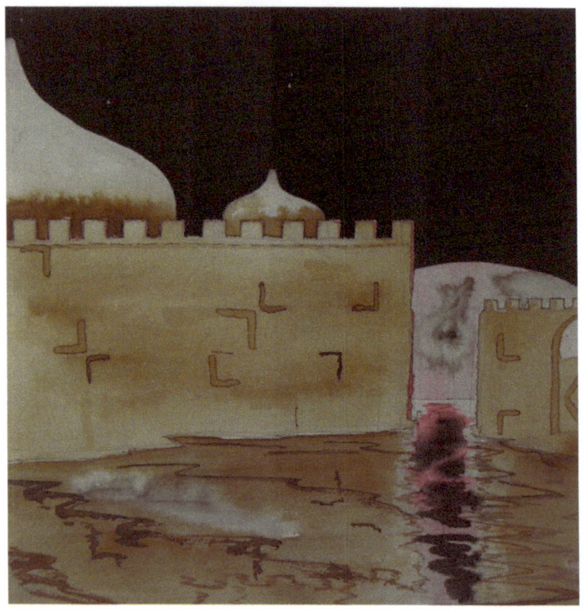

▲ 5 **and stir,**
Width x Height x Depth: 30 x 30 cm
Medium; Inks on Paper.
Additional Information: From 'Vinyl Cities and other Stories Exhibition'.

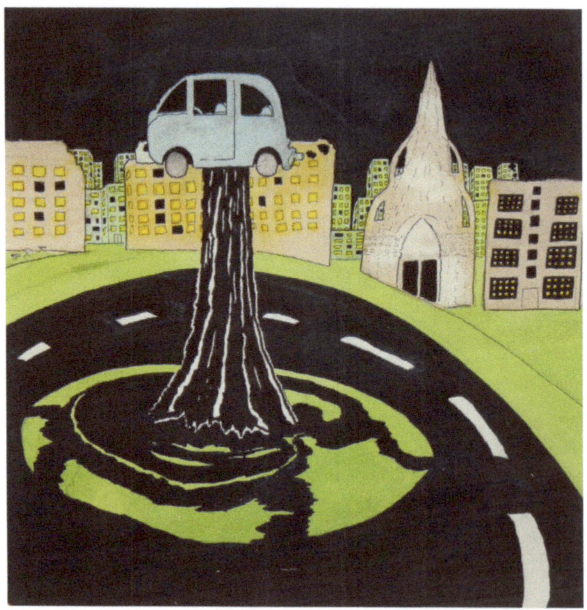

▲ 6 **while other things couldn't.**
Width x Height x Depth: 30 x 30 cm
Medium; Inks on Paper.
Additional Information: From 'Vinyl Cities and other Stories Exhibition'.

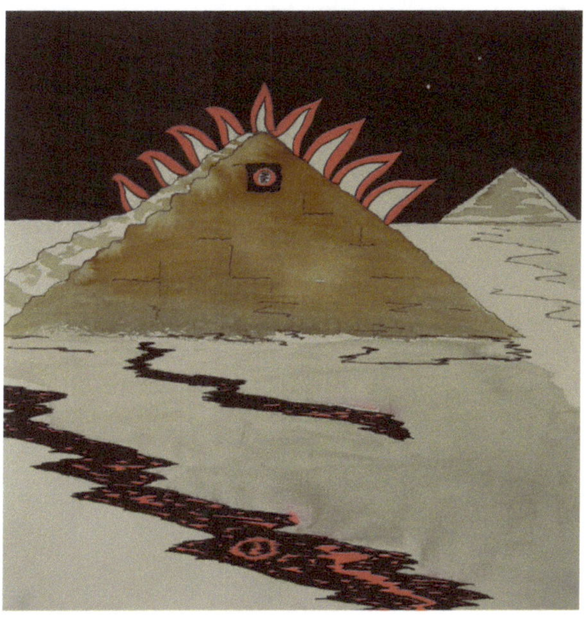

▲ **After the pyramids became flatter,**
7 Width x Height x Depth: 30 x 30 cm
Medium; Inks on Paper.
Additional Information: From 'Vinyl Cities and other Stories Exhibition'.

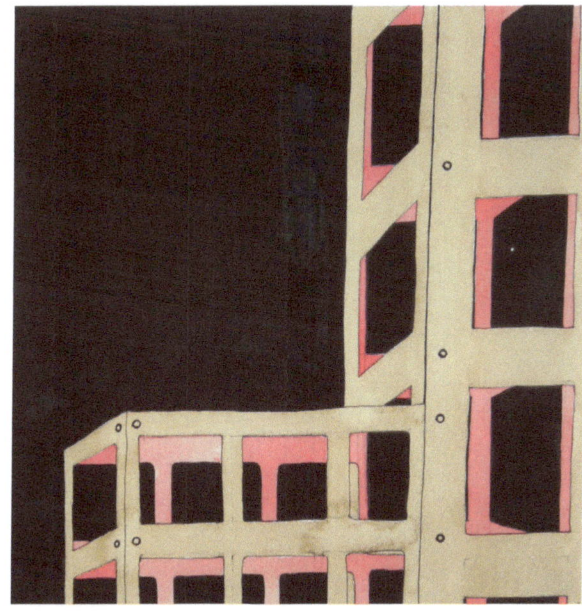

▲ **the city became a**
8 Width x Height x Depth: 30 x 30 cm
Medium; Inks on Paper.
Additional Information: From 'Vinyl Cities and other Stories Exhibition'.

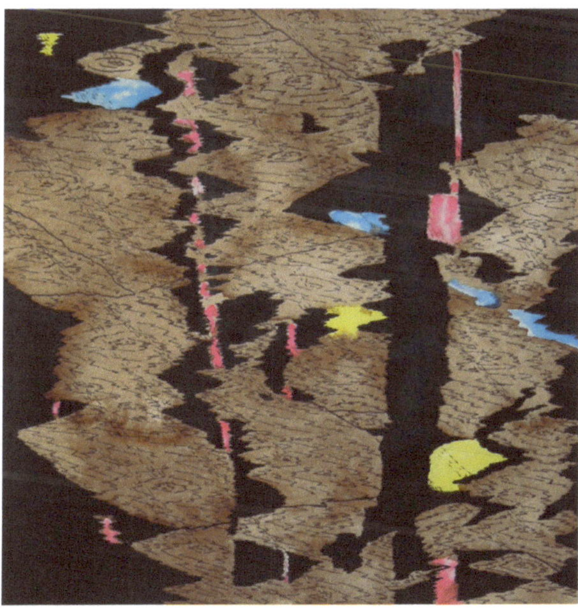

▲ **home.**
9 Width x Height x Depth: 30 x 30 cm
Medium; Inks on Paper.
Additional Information: From 'Vinyl Cities and other Stories Exhibition'.

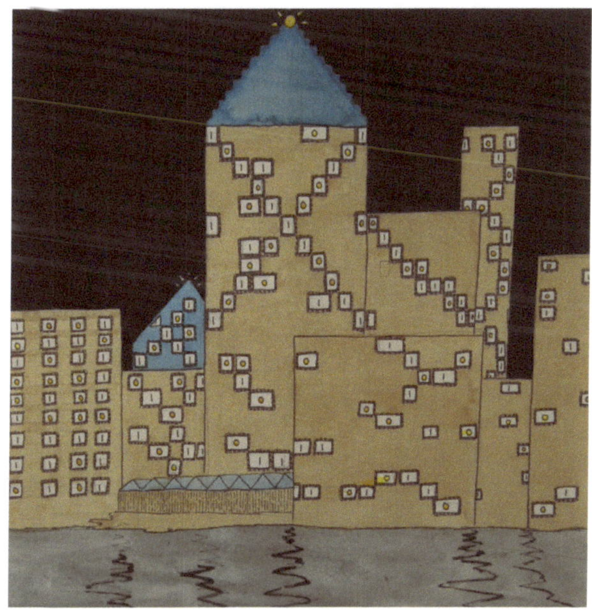

▲ **On the banks of the rivers Thames**
10 Width x Height x Depth: 30 x 30 cm
Medium; Inks on Paper.
Additional Information: From 'Vinyl Cities and other Stories Exhibition'.

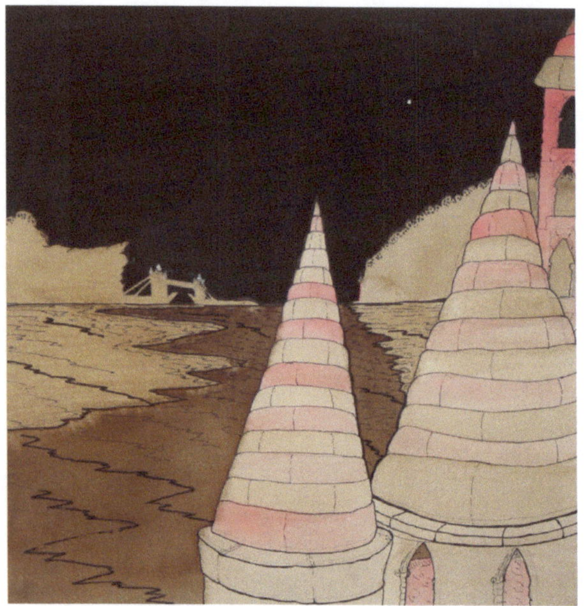

▲ 11 **and Spree**
Width x Height x Depth: 30 x 30 cm
Medium; Inks on Paper.
Additional Information: From 'Vinyl Cities and other Stories Exhibition'.

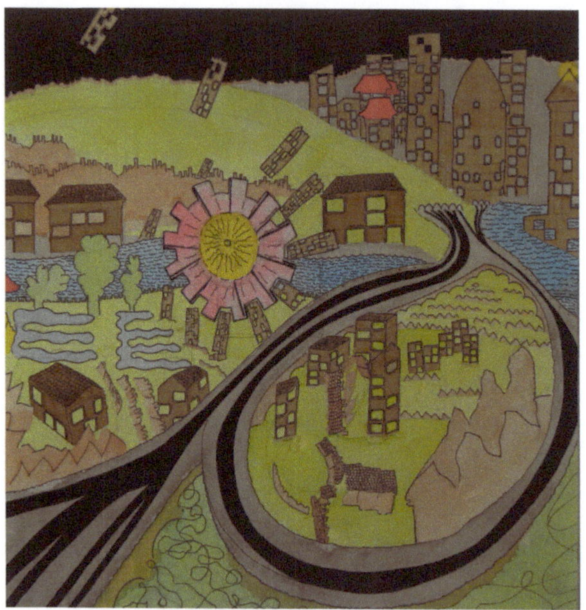

▲ 12 **things began to change**
Width x Height x Depth: 30 x 30 cm
Medium; Inks on Paper.
Additional Information: From 'Vinyl Cities and other Stories Exhibition'.

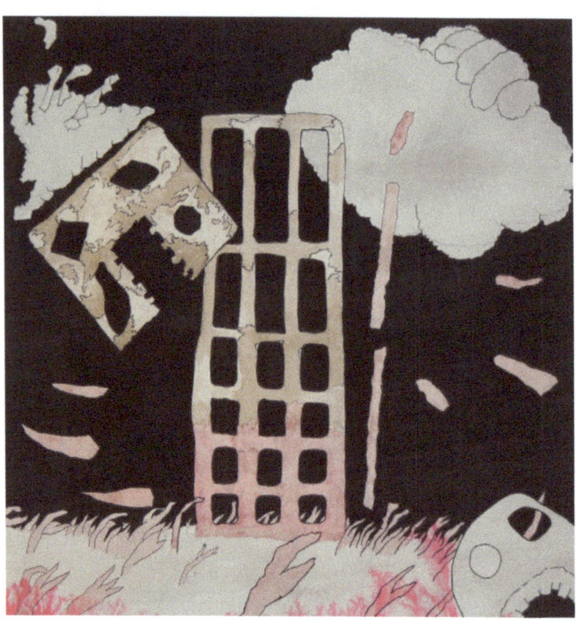

▲ 13 **as ways of thinking**
Width x Height x Depth: 30 x 30 cm
Medium; Inks on Paper.
Additional Information: From 'Vinyl Cities and other Stories Exhibition'.

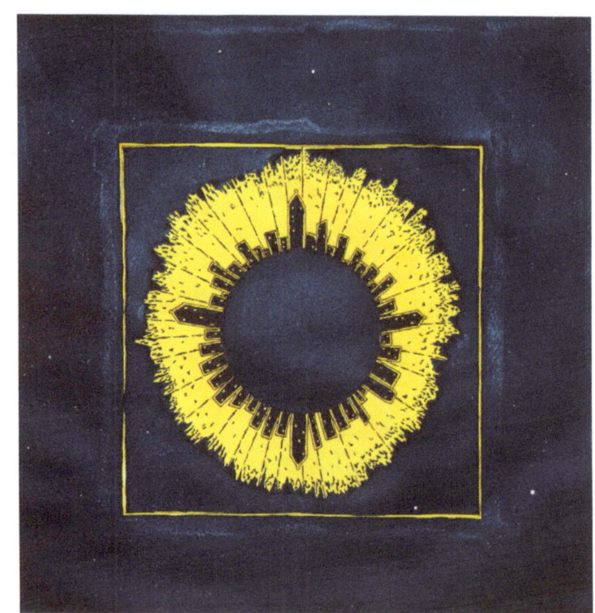

▲ 14 **evolved.**
Width x Height x Depth: 30 x 30 cm
Medium; Inks on Paper.
Additional Information: From 'Vinyl Cities and other Stories Exhibition'.

Biographies

Yair Meshoulam Art School: Royal College of Art MA (Painting) 1986-88, Ruskin School of Drawing & Fine Art, BFA Oxford University Scholar 1982-5

Exhibitions:

2014: Open Studio, Dulwich Open Studios, ACME Studios, Carlew House, West Norwood.

2013: Solo Show 'The Texture of Consciousness' Weekend Gallery, Charlottenburg, Berlin; Curating 'Christine Kühn 1953-2011 – Installations in Changing Times' Kesselhaus Museum, Lichtenberg, Berlin; Installation of photographic show 'Christine Kühn (1953-2013), Weekend Gallery, Charlottenburg, Berlin.
Open Studio, Dulwich Open Studios, ACME Studios, Carlew House, West Norwood; Art-Trail 'Collectables' 5th Avenue, Brixton Village Market, London

2012: Group Show, Portico Gallery, Knights Hill, West Norwood, London.
Two Person Show 'Arab Spring' Project The Weekend Gallery, Charlottenburg, Berlin.
'Curious' 'Spirit Bird Boxes', Art Trail, West Norwood Cemetery, London;
'Curious' Works on Paper, Portico Gallery, Knights Hill, West Norwood, London;
Co Curator 'Christine Kühn 1953-2011' Memorial Show at The Weekend Gallery, Charlottenburg, Berlin; Open Studio, ACME Studios, Carlew House, West Norwood, London;' Wallpapered Furniture' West Norwood 'Feast' Festival & DoopoDoopo Forest Hill, London; Songwriting workshop Jerwood Art Space, Union St, London SE1 part of 'Now I gotta reason' events, with Steve Ounanlan & Pete Astor.

2011: Group Show, St Edmund Hall, Oxford University, Oxford; Dulwich Open Studios (ACME - Carlew House West Norwood);

2010: Late at Tate Britain, London. 'Shards of Utopia' Lecture/Performance/Music with Steve Ounanlan; Barbican in Ron Arad Show Lecture/Performance/Music with Steve Ounanian;
Stoke Newington International Airport, London. Lecture/Performance/Music with Steve Ounanian; LondoNewcastle Project Space, Redchurch St E2 'Subverting Belief' Lecture/Performance/ Music with Steve Ounanian, curated Cecilia Wee/ Neville Brody; The Incredible Trip to The Holy Mountain, Arts Admin Toynbee Whitechapel, London. Lecture/Performance/Music with Steve Ounanain: Group Show Elm Green School, West Norwood, London.

2009: Group Show Lambeth Open London; Video Web project Bureau de Change' Bank of Hope http://www.stevenlevon.com/?cat=16

2008: Two Person Show 'Wall Street', Bureau de Change, Shunt, London Bridge, London; Urban Arts, Brixton, London.

2007: Open Studio ASC 246 Stockwell Road Brixton London.

2006: Group Show 'Technology of Enchantment' Gallery CVA @ Menier Chocolate Factory London; 'Around the Houses Two' Brixton, London.

2005: Group Show 198 Gallery Brixton London; Group Show IJAYA (International Jewish Artists of the Year Awards)
Ben Uri Gallery @ Tram Studios Camden Town, London; Open Studio ASC 246 Stockwell Road Brixton London.

2004: Open Studio ASC 246 Stockwell Road, Brixton, London;
Group Show, 198 Gallery, Brixton, London.

2003: Selected Group 'Director's Choice' - Work to be purchased by the Ben Uri Collection, London.

2003: Selected Group Show, Limmud, Conference, Bromley College, Kent.

2002: Selected Group Show, 291 Gallery Hackney, London.

2001: Selected Group Show, Ben Uri, Jewish Artist of the Year, Angel, London;
Selected Group Show, 'Secret', RCA, London Bowieart.com/Time Out.

2000: Selected Group Show, 'Contemporary Ceremonial Art', Succah, Jewish Museum, Camden Town, London.

1999: Selected Group Show, 'Jewish Magic and Mysticism', Jewish Museum, Camden Town, London. House Show, Brixton, London.

1998: Solo Show 'Androids, Robots and Golems' Trevelyan College, Durham University, Durham;
Solo Show Works on Paper 1988-1998 Ozten Zeki Gallery, Brompton Cross, London; Group Show Ozten Zeki Gallery, Brompton Cross, London; Open Studio Show, Parade Mews Studios, Tulse Hill, London.

1997: Solo Show 'Robots', Ozten Zeki Gallery, Brompton Cross, London; Group Show, Ozten Zeki Gallery, Brompton Cross, London; Group Show, Connoisseur Gallery, London.

1996: Two Person Show, Städtische Gallerie Haus Seel, Public Art Gallery, Siegen, Germany;
Whitechapel Open Studios, ACME Childers Street Open, New Cross, London; Group Show, Fitch's Ark, Little Venice, London; Group Show, 'Beyond England' - Internationally Exhibited Art RCA Graduates, Hockney Gallery, London; Group Show, Art Connoisseur Gallery, Marylebone, London.

1995: Two Person Show, Curated by Julia Weiner, Boston Consultancy, Mayfair, London;
Single Stall, Alternative Art Market, Alternative Arts, Spitalfields Market, London; Ben Uri Open, Ben Uri Gallery, Dean Street, Soho, London; Two Person Show, 'As Above, So Below', Ben Uri Gallery, Soho, London; Group Show, House of William Blake, South Molton St., London; Group Show, Atrium Gallery, Whiteley's, Queensway, London.

1994: Berlin/London Exchange Group Show, British Council, Bahnhof Westend, Berlin;
Ben Uri Open, Dean Street, Soho, London; Group Show, Atrium Gallery, London.

1993: Whitechapel Open Studios, 'Diagrams of Splendour', Childers Street, London;
Ben Uri Open, Ben Uri Gallery, Dean Street, Soho, London; Group Show, Slaughterhouse Gallery, Smithfields, London; Group Show, Smith's Gallery, Covent Garden, London;
Group Show, Hyde Park Gallery, London; Group Show, The Gallery, Mayfair, London.

1992: Selected for Whitechapel Open, Whitechapel Gallery, London;
Group Show, London Connection', Kassel (during Documenta),Germany;
Group Show, 'Bloom', European Outposts, Spitalfields, London;
Two Person Show, Gallery 47, Bloomsbury, London;
Whitechapel Open Studios, Tower Bridge Studios, London;

1991: Two Person Show, Ozten Zeki Gallery, Brompton Cross, London;
Three Person Show, Gallery Dagmar, Dulwich, London.
Group Show, 'Utopias', Gallery Dagmar, Dulwich, London Gallery, London
Group Show 'Pictures on the Railings', Dagmar/ Dulwich Picture Gallery, London;
Group Show 'East Meets West', Smith's Gallery, Covent Garden, London.

1990: Portobello Open, Tabernacle Gallery, Portobello Road, London.

1989: Selected for Whitechapel Open, Whitechapel Gallery, London;
Three Person Show, Gallery Dagmar, Dulwich, London;

1988: Degree Show, Painting Department, Royal College of Art, London.

Awards:

1982-1985 Scholarship, St. Edmund Hall/Ruskin, Oxford University.
Collections: Public - Sure Start, Lambeth Education London; Oxfordshire Health Authority, John Radcliffe Hospital; St. Edmund Hall, Oxford University; Private -Simmonds; Dr Brian Whitton, Micro Biologist (Durham University) & Art Historian, Author of British Surrealist 'Tunnard'; Chandris.

Teaching:

Winchester School of Art, Foundation Course, Visiting Lecturer. Winchester School of Art, Art History Course; Visiting Lecturer. Summer School Robin Child Norwich, Wiltshire, Cambridge; Workshops Rosendale Primary School, South London Artweek.

Publications:

2013: Kaltblut Magazine. September Issue. Review of "Texture of Consciousness' Show Weekend Gallery Berlin.

2000: Succah Panels–Jewish Ceremonial Art, Jewish Museum ISBN 953312910

1999: Contributor, 'Fold, Newspaper of the Unconscious ISBN 1466-4089

1998: Catalogue Solo Durham Show, 'Androids, Robots & Golems', Meshoulam/Reid/Weiner ISBN 0953312909.1997: Jewish Chronicle, 'Making their mark, up and coming Jewish Artists', Julia Weiner. 1996: Siegen Zietung Newspaper; Westfalen Rundschau; Westfalen Post; Reviews of Seigen Show, Germany.1995: Catalogue Ben Uri Gallery 'As Above, so Below' – Images inspired by the Kabbalah GLR Radio Interview; Jewish London item on Kabbalah, discussion & review of Ben Uri Show; Ham & High Newspaper Review of Ben Uri Show, 'Magic and Morality', LindaTalbot.1994: Catalogue British Council Show in Berlin; 'Arrival'. Der Tagespiegel, Berlin Newspaper Review, Katrin Bettina Muller.1993: Catalogue Childers Street Show, 'Diagrams of Splendour, Paintings from the Zohar' Kabbalah;

1992: Catalogue Gallery 47 Show, 'Little Flowers of St Francis'; Catalogue Ozten Zeki Gallery, 'Biblical Paintings' ;Guardian Newspaper Whitechapel Open Review, Whitechapel Gallery, 'Under Eastern Eyes' Tim Hilton; New Statesman. Whitechapel Open Studios Review, David Langsam.

Video links:

2014: 'Yair : I am a painter' Directed by Jose Silver
https://www.youtube.com/watch?v=q7D5O8CEunY
http://vimeo.com/94775773

Websites:
www.yairmeshoulam.com
www.textureofconsciousness.com
www.wallpaperhangers.org.uk

'Locked in Syndrome' contributors:

Karl-Heinz Pantke was born in Braunschweig, West Germany, in 1955. He received a Diploma in 1985 and then a Ph.D. in 1990 in Physics from the Technische Universität in Berlin, where he was a research fellow. From 1990 to 1993 he held a research fellowship at the Odense University, Denmark, funded by the Danish Natural Science Research Council Fellowship. The next year he returned to Germany and became Assistant Professor in Physics at the Technische Universitat in Dresden specialising in the field of ultrafast processes in semiconductors. In 1995, he suffered a stroke followed by Locked-in-Syndrome, and his scientific publication work went on hold as he recovered from Locked-in-Syndrome (LiS) with the innovative physiotherapy work being developed in Berlin. In 2000 he founded the organisation LiS, together with his partner, the artist Christine Kühn, and other sufferers of LiS. He became President of this organization and from 2005 his scientific publications recommenced. After Christine's death in 2011, he became the Chair of the *Christine Kühn foundation for the improvement of the living conditions of patients with the Locked-in-Syndrome.*

Yair first met Karl-Heinz and Christine, when she was studying on a DAAD one year scholarship at the Royal College of Art in London in 1986, and subsequently in a DAAD-RCA group show with the British Council in the Bahnhof Westend in Berlin in 1994, and later in 1996 in a two person show in Seigen. After Christine's death, Yair helped Karl-Heinz curate and install shows of her work at The Weekend Gallery in 2012 and in the following year at the Kesselhaus Museum, and also worked with the English text for the catalogues.

Karl-Heinz's co-authors for this contribution are Linda Loschinski and Julia Szymetzko, and Yair knows them through Karl-Heinz.

Linda Loschinski was born in Berlin in 1988, and received a BA degree in Philosophy-Neuroscience-Cognition from the Otto-von-Guericke Universität in Magdeburg in 2013, following on with an MSc in Medical Psychology at the Steinbeis-Hochschule in Berlin.

Julia Szymetzko was born in 1985. After studying German and Scandinavian literature at Humboldt-Universität zu Berlin, she gained an MA in European Contemporary Literature focusing on Literature and Medicine, particularly Jean-Dominique Bauby's autobiography 'The Diving Bell and the Butterfly', and is following up with a PhD on autobiography and illness in literature.

Organisations

The LIS (Locked-in-Syndrome) e.V. non profit company was founded in 2000 by Christine Kühn, Karl-Heinz Pantke and others. It has members with the Locked-in-Syndrome throughout Europe. The headquarter of the organisation is situated at the Elizabeth Psychiatric Hospital in Lichtenberg, Berlin. KEH (Krankenhaus Königin Elisabeth Herzberge) - Haus 30, Herzbergstr. 79, 10365 Berlin.

The Christine Kühn foundation was founded in 2013 with the last will of Christine Kühn, who died in 2011. The foundation tries to improve the living conditions of patients with the Locked-in-Syndrome.

Mark Fielding and Yair Meshoulam are family friends from Brixton, and is one of the few people Yair knows whose day job is Philosopher, apart from AJ Ayer who was his uncle.

Mark Fielding is a founding member of The London School of Philosophy and has taught at UCL, Birkbeck College, The Open University, and The University of Greenwich. He holds degrees from the University of Manchester and UCL. His principle interests are in the areas of Philosophy and Film, contemporary political thought, 20th Century French and German Philosophy, and Philosophy and Biology. He has recently been working on books on Philosophy and Horror and the nature of political utopias in the contemporary world.

Robert Silman was a close friend of Yair's late mother Felicity Meshoulam.

He obtained a degree in Philosophy at the Sorbonne where he was a student of Jean-Francois Lyotard and Jacques Derrida. He returned to London and became a medical doctor before full time medical research at St Bartholomew's Hospital where he authored scores of research publications principally on the role of the pituitary hormones ACTH and endorphin in pregnancy and parturition, and the pineal hormone melatonin in growth and puberty. More recently he has addressed the problem of how to filter for quality on the web, in particular how to promote artists of talent amidst the immensity of the web and has a US patent, *A Quality Filter for the Internet.*

Jacques Naoum was born in Tripoli, Lebanon in 1938, and has been a resident in Berlin since 1963, where he studied Theatre and Romance languages, and works for the press and radio, and is the author of 'Rathaus-Erzahlung' (Brandes & Apsel, 2006). In the 1980's, with a group of friends including Christine Kühn, Jacques founded an art project space called *The Weekend Gallery*, near the Museum Berggruen in Charlottenburg. Yair has shown a number of times at *The Weekend Gallery*, and has set up a sister space in London.

Ruth Fainlight and her husband Alan Sillitoe were friends of Yair's mother, Felicity Meshoulam, while they were living in Mallorca in the 1950s. Indeed it was Felicity who transported Alan Sillitoe's short story "The Loneliness of the Long Distance Runner" to Alan's publisher in London.

Ruth was born in New York City and has lived in England since the age of 15, mostly in London. She lived in Spain for four years in her 20s, and has spent long periods in France and Morocco. Her first poetry collection, Cages, was published in 1966. She was Poet in Residence at Vanderbilt University, Nashville, Tennessee, in 1985 and 1990. She was Writing Tutor (for libretti) at the Performing Arts Labs, International Opera and Music Theatre Labs in the UK in 1997-99. Her New & Collected Poems (Bloodaxe Books, 2010) covers work written over 50 years, drawing on over a dozen books as well as a whole new collection, translations and libretti. Four of those collections were originally published by Bloodaxe, including Sugar-Paper Blue (1997), which was shortlisted for the Whitbread Poetry Award. Other collections were published by Macmillan, Hutchinson and Sinclair-Stevenson. Ruth Fainlight's collections of short stories include Daylife and Nightlife (Andre Deutsch, 1971) and Dr Clock's Last Case and Other Stories (Virago, 1994). As a poet, short-story writer and translator, she has contributed to many anthologies. Her own work has been translated into Portuguese, French, Spanish, Italian and Romanian, and she has herself published translations from the Portuguese of the poetry of Sophia de Mello Breyner, and from the Spanish of several Latin American poets represented in her New & Collected Poems. She has also written four libretti: The Dancer Hotoke (1991), a chamber opera with music by Erika Fox, performed as part of the Royal Opera's 'Garden Venture' in 1991 and shortlisted for the Laurence Olivier Award for Outstanding Achievement in Opera; The European Story (based on her poem of the same title, 1993), also commissioned by the Royal Opera House; and Bedlam Britannica, which was commissioned by Channel 4 Television for the series War Cries in 1995; and The Bride in Her Grave. Her translation (with Robert J. Littman) of The Theban Plays by Sophocles (Oedipus the King, Oedipus at Colonus and Antigone) was published in 2009 in the Johns Hopkins University Press's New Translations from Antiquity series. She has received the Hawthorden Award and the Cholmondeley Award for Poetry, and is a Fellow of the Royal Society of Literature. An audio CD, Ruth Fainlight Reading from her Poems, was issued by The Poetry Archive in 2008.

www.ingramcontent.com/pod-product-compliance
Lightning Source LLC
LaVergne TN
LVHW070126110826
845147LV00002B/195

9781910133057